T0315507

Where We Stand

DJAMILA RIBEIRO

Where
We Stand

Translated from the Portuguese by
Padma Viswanathan

Foreword by Chimamanda Ngozi Adichie

A MARGELLOS
WORLD REPUBLIC OF LETTERS BOOK

Yale UNIVERSITY PRESS | NEW HAVEN & LONDON

English translation copyright © 2024 by Padma Viswanathan.
Originally published in Portuguese as *Lugar de fala,* copyright © Djamila Ribeiro, 2019.
Foreword copyright © 2024 by Chimamanda Ngozi Adichie.

Yale University Press books may be purchased in quantity for educational, business, or promotional use. For information, please e-mail sales.press@yale.edu (U.S. office) or sales@yaleup.co.uk (U.K. office).

Set in Source Serif type by Motto Publishing Services.
Printed in the United States of America.

Library of Congress Control Number: 2023948636
ISBN 978-0-300-26964-2 (hardcover : alk. paper)

A catalogue record for this book is available from the British Library.
This paper meets the requirements of ANSI/NISO Z39.48-1992 (Permanence of Paper).

10 9 8 7 6 5 4 3 2 1

For Thulane, a piece of me and of the world

With gratitude to Odé, my Orisha, for everything

Special thanks to Brenno Tardelli,
for partnership in writing, life, and love

Contents

Foreword

Chimamanda Ngozi Adichie

How many times have I been asked, as Djamila Ribeiro recounts, which identity matters more to me, Black or Woman? Ribeiro's response is humorous but no less insightful for being so—one does not decide what time of the day to be Black and what time to be a Woman.

To be a Black woman in a world that stigmatizes certain people on account of race and gender is to instinctively understand the inherently nuanced nature of identity. Our very existence as Black women is a repudiation of any attempt to simplify identity. Ribeiro suggests that the discourse around identity must necessarily be ongoing, always alert to complexity, and never assume that categories are "fixed or stable." But, thankfully, she does not sacrifice clarity in the name of complexity. Identity is never simple, and the existence of Black women in particular demonstrates this.

However, this complexity should not provide a convenient reason for inaction, leading to such conclusions as "It's all so complicated, nothing can be done," or, even more dangerous, "We cannot focus on identity because it's so complicated, so we should talk only of our shared humanity." Of course our humanity is shared, but Ribeiro understands how easily these kinds of platitudes can lead, as she so beautifully puts it, to a "universality that excludes." It is imperative, therefore, to focus on the intricate specificities of identity, while having as a larger framework the acknowledgment of an overarching complexity.

It is courageous—though it should not and would not be considered "courageous" if we lived in an equal world—of Ribeiro to name the obstacles to real conversations which can lead to real change. In her elucidation of the idea of the *speaking place,* she boldly states that "groups that have always held power are discomfited by the advance of a discourse on rights by minority groups." It is this discomfort, this unwillingness to engage, this reluctance to change on the part of societally powerful groups that ultimately burdens minority groups with stereotypes. A group long deprived and dehumanized might, for example, be said to be hostile, and that label is not questioned, even though it came as a result of the group's attempts to address its own deprivation and dehumanization. It is therefore logical for Ribeiro to write that what is being questioned—and should be questioned—is the "legitimacy conferred upon those belonging to the group located in power."

Ribeiro's exploration of the idea of individual experience is crucial. She does not dismiss the value of individual experience, but she rejects its primacy in the discourse of minority groups' rights. Individual experience cannot be the focus, because that experience is largely mitigated by the individual's membership in a group, and also because focusing on the micro-level can be an easy way of dismissing a group's dispossession by highlighting the rare members of that group who have fared better despite their oppression.

This book could be read first as a primer on Black feminist thought, the different permutations on the status of women whose lives are shaped by "the double bind of the colonial and male gaze." Black women are different because they have often been cast in the role of objects, while "a variable status permits both white women and Black men potentially to emplace themselves as subjects." This book could also be read as a courageous call to arms, a lucid argument for "a different starting point."

What is most appealing to me, however, is its rootedness in the practical, the everyday lives of actual human beings. *Where We Stand* is intent on, perhaps even immersed in, feminist theory, but only insofar as it can light the path toward understanding and improving lived realities. It is never theory for its own sake. I hope many readers will come to this intellectually curious and clear-eyed exploration of identity, of Black women's intellectual thought, and of the lives of Black women.

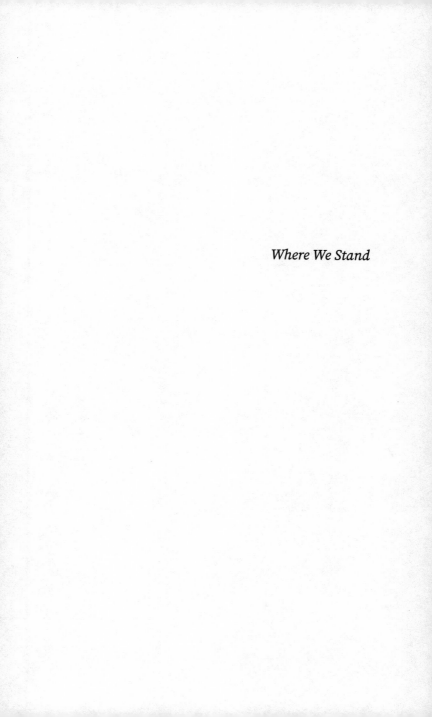

Where We Stand

Introduction

To see my first book, *Where We Stand,* translated into English for American readers is a huge pleasure, after my years of working to transform the Brazilian publishing landscape. Publishing is power, and in Brazil, as in the United States, publishing is an industry in dire need of transformation. Amid racial reckonings across the Americas and beyond, it is crucial to name the relationship between the publishing industry and the exercise of cultural, political, and social influence, and to explore the ways in which the dynamics of this relationship often align with racial and gender-based inequities. But before telling the story of my mission to publish and promote Black thinkers and writers in Brazil, I would like to share my own journey as a Black intellectual and publisher, and describe what motivated me to seek to bring about change in this sphere of Brazilian cultural life.

I was born in 1980 in São Paulo, and spent most of my life in Santos, a coastal town in the state of São Paulo, where my father was born. I am the daughter of Joaquim José Ribeiro dos Santos, a longshoreman who worked at the Santos port, and Erani Benedita dos Santos, a homemaker who worked as a domestic cleaner until she married my dad. I'm the youngest of four, with two older brothers and an older

sister. My father was an activist in the Black liberation movement, a union organizer, and one of the founders of the
Communist Party in Santos. He read to us, gave us books,
and insisted that we get good grades in school. From early
on, he impressed on us the importance of race- and class-
consciousness. He made us go to protests, participate in social movements, and attend the theater; he even enrolled us
in chess lessons. I was reading fluently by age six, and at
eight I won the Santos bronze medal in chess. Although we
were working-class kids, we had access to a quality education—and to critical consciousness-raising—from the time
we were small.

While our father encouraged us to study, our mother
washed our uniforms, combed our hair, and above all taught
us to walk with our heads held high. When I was eight, she
initiated me into *candomblé,* a religious tradition of African
origin, and she modeled the spirituality that would form
the bedrock of my identity. My father put us in an English
school; he said education was the only way for us to transcend the obstacles imposed by racism, so he worked hard
to make sure we had access to it, though he struggled to pay
our school fees. I was the only Black girl in my class for years.
When we returned to school after holidays, my classmates
would talk excitedly about their trips to Disneyland or Europe. I spent my holidays at my grandmother's house in the
Brazilian interior or at a beach town near Santos. I learned
to live within this paradox: I studied at one of the best English schools, paid for by scrimping, but I came home alone
on the bus; I played chess with white kids but had to tutor for
extra money. I grew up doing this *ginga,* the back-and-forth
dance of capoeira.

My parents had both died by the time I was twenty-two: my mother in May 2001, and my father in November 2002. I suddenly found myself an orphan, forced to navigate life alongside my siblings. At the time, I was studying journalism at a private college in Santos and barely managing to make ends meet. A few years earlier, when I was nineteen, an acquaintance of my mother's had hired me as a general services assistant, cleaning buildings and fetching coffee. I often arrived at my university classes smelling of bleach. Even though I had a stronger résumé than the young women working in the company's administrative office, even though I knew English and was well spoken, I was offered only menial work. When I told them, my parents were incensed: my mother, who had been a domestic worker for years, did not want her daughter "scrubbing toilets for white people." My father would not speak to me for months after I began working as a cleaner, saying he had "worked himself to death carrying sacks of sugar on his back" so I could have a better future. After my parents died, to honor their hopes, I decided to investigate other possibilities.

I had begun working in a Black feminist organization called the Black Women's Cultural Center, a place that proved vital to my political education. There, as I helped put together seminars and discussions about Black Brazil, I gradually came to understand myself as a feminist. What was most significant, however, was access to the center's library, where I encountered the Black women writers who changed my life. At twenty-one, I read Toni Morrison's *The Bluest Eye* for the first time, and a new world opened up to me. I was barely able to pay for college, but working at the organization strengthened my self-esteem and sense of belonging.

When I was in my third year of college, I became pregnant and dropped out of school. Thulane was born in 2005, and her father and I decided to live together and raise her in the best possible way. As a Black family, we considered it very important to do everything we could for our daughter. I loved being a mother, but I did not conform to conventional expectations of motherhood. After all, I had been raised to have choices; now, I found myself without many prospects for a life outside the home. In 2007, determined to continue my education, I decided to take the philosophy entrance exam for the Federal University of São Paulo. I passed the exam, but I lived in Santos, and the campus was in Guarulhos, two hours away by car. Thulane was three years old, and those around me strongly discouraged me from continuing my studies. One day at home, in a fit of rage, I said, "My grandmother wasn't able to study and neither was my mother. I'm breaking this cycle now." I did, but it was hard. I was twenty-eight at the time and teaching in a state school to support myself. Despite my guilt, I decided to continue my studies, to show my daughter an alternative vision of motherhood. Though just a child, she was much more understanding than the adults.

My time in the degree program was difficult. I was taught exclusively European philosophy, developed by white men. I wanted to study Black and female philosophers, but I encountered intense resistance to their methods. In response, some peers and I decided to form a study group on race, gender, and sexuality, and we began organizing events at the university. In 2010, while doing research, I discovered that there was a group of researchers who studied Simone de Beauvoir's thinking and organized annual conferences on her work. My English was rusty after years without practice, but I decided to translate a research paper I had written into English and apply to attend the Simone de Beauvoir Society conference. To my complete surprise, my paper was accepted, but if I wanted to go, I would have to pay my travel and accommodation expenses: the conference was in Eugene, at the University of Oregon. Though it was a difficult process, I managed to get an American visa; and though I was scared, I went. I'd never traveled outside Brazil, and I remember watching how people acted in the airplane and airport so I could imitate them. Upon arriving in Oregon, I was welcomed by many of the academics at the conference, even though I was only in the third year of my undergraduate program in philosophy and the great majority of the conference attendees were college professors. I presented my paper, which received positive attention. Margaret Simons, a renowned Beauvoir scholar, for example, gave me all the books the Simone de Beauvoir Society had published. She encouraged and supported me, and I returned to Brazil feeling validated and inspired in my intellectual pursuits. I decided to persevere and follow my intellectual interests, in spite of the fact that many of my professors regarded Beauvoir simply as "Sartre's 'wife.'"

After I graduated, I chose to continue my education and pursue a graduate degree, focusing my research on feminist philosophy. In 2014, I participated in another conference organized by the Simone de Beauvoir Society, this time in St. Louis, and once again I relied on the generosity of the professors, who debated and discussed my graduate research. In

2015, at age thirty-five, I defended my master's thesis and re-solved to do whatever I could to right the epistemic wrongs I had endured over my years in the academy.

In 2016, I was appointed assistant secretary for human rights in the city of São Paulo. By this time, I was reason-ably well known as a writer. Called on to help in the wake of a publisher's internal reckoning over their dearth of Black voices, I emailed the scholar and activist Angela Davis and invited her to collaborate with the publisher. Davis's classic work *Women, Race & Class* had been published in English in the eighties, but other than informal translations by collec-tives, it had not been published in Brazil. She accepted my offer, and I wrote the foreword for the Brazilian edition and helped to promote the book—so successfully that it became one of the year's best sellers in Brazil. The publisher refused to pay me anything for my foreword or my efforts in pro-moting the book, and though I was thrilled with its much-deserved success, I realized that I could not be dependent on organizations led by white people who did not under-stand the need for Black protagonism on a deep level, and who were not committed to the cause but only looking for profit.[1]

I wanted to use the visibility I had gained to make oth-ers more visible—a collective path was the only course that made sense to me. That was when I got the idea to create a series of books featuring exclusively Black writers: in 2017, the Plural Feminisms Collection was born.

The objective of the Plural Feminisms Collection is to publish and popularize the thinking of Black authors. We have already issued fourteen titles, and nearly all the au-thors were previously unknown to the majority of the Brazilian reading public. Many of these thinkers published their first books with us.

According to research by the University of Brasilia's Contemporary Literature Study Group, between the years 1965 and 2014, 70 percent of works issued by major Brazilian publishers were written by men, 90 percent of whom were white.[2] This statistic says a lot about the Brazilian publishing market, especially considering that 56 percent of the Brazilian population identifies as Black or Afro-Brazilian. There had certainly been crucial Black-led publishing initiatives before Plural Feminisms, but given the ongoing marginalization of Brazilian Black intellectuals, I felt strongly that much more needed to be done. I conceived a series of topics and invited Black thinkers to write on them. My study of the market showed me that we needed a strategy to ensure the books' accessibility and activate public interest. For this reason, I resolved that the volumes should contain plain, explanatory language, be affordably priced, and have bibliographies comprised mostly of Black authors, so that they would also function as a way to break down the invisibility of older generations of Black intellectuals. We organized launches in public venues throughout the country. Breaking with publishers' traditional focus on large urban centers, we launched our books in less well resourced areas, including the outskirts of cities and the Brazilian interior. Coming from a Black working-class family, I know that bookstores can be intimidating; a whole class of people feel they don't belong in such places. So we organized launch events in libraries, on beaches, in schools, in community and cultural centers, and on the streets.

At each author's initial launch, we handed out free books

to the first hundred people who arrived. We featured local musicians, served food, hosted a huge celebration. Then, toting more books, we traveled all over the country, talking with the people we encountered and working to popularize critical ideas developed by Black thinkers.

At the first launch event for *Lugar de fala* (the Brazilian original of *Where We Stand*) in December 2017, more than two thousand people showed up—so many that the authorities had to shut down the main street in the well-known neighborhood of Lapa, in Rio de Janeiro. It was there that I saw the project's full potential and understood the power of a public mobilized around reading. Another two thousand people came out to attend the launch in the northern state of Acre, three thousand in the northeastern city of Fortaleza, thousands more in the southeastern city of Belo Horizonte. Since then, the project has rapidly expanded. We have given thousands of books to public schools, collectives, community libraries, and cultural centers throughout the country.

In 2018, I met Lizandra Magon, the feminist publisher responsible for Editora Jandaira, an independent publishing house with a solid reputation and good visibility at literary festivals and in bookstores. We entered into a co-publishing agreement for the Plural Feminisms Collection: sharing costs, strategies, and profits. This cooperation was unprecedented: until that point, all the publishers who approached us had wanted us to turn the project over to them. Jandaira was the only publisher that respected our authority to determine content and publish the books in the way we chose. The co-publishing launch drew a crowd of over three thousand in São Paulo. The Collection's sales shot through the roof. That same year, as a tribute to the trailblazing Black

Brazilian feminist, I launched the Sueli Carneiro editorial imprint with Jandaira, under the same co-publishing terms; this imprint would publish longer works (the books in the Plural Feminisms Collection were pocket editions). I published *Sueli Carneiro: Notes on a Life* to give younger generations access to this major figure's thinking. In 2020, I published *Quilombola Women,* a book that brings together contributions by eighteen women in various quilombola communities, settlements founded generations ago by people who escaped slavery. This was also unprecedented: it was the first time that a collective of quilombola women had spoken back to the centers of power from where they stood. We created our Little Carneiro children's imprint, aimed at publishing works for children and adolescents, and brought out *Betha, the Black Ballerina.* In 2021, following a call for proposals, we selected articles written by Black scholars on overlooked historical Black figures. These were published in the volume *Making History: Black Figures Made Visible.* In 2020, we inaugurated the series Okan Dudu, aimed at publishing works on African-derived religions, with *Axé: Power of Fulfillment.* That same year, I saw a longtime dream realized: we opened the Plural Feminisms Space, a house in southern São Paulo where we host book launches, run a library and research room, and offer free legal, psychological, and dental services to vulnerable women. In partnership with Rosangela Riggo House, São Paulo's first shelter for women fleeing domestic abuse, we created group therapy both for the women using the shelter's services and for the Rosangela Riggo House staff under the rubric of the new program "Caring for Those Who Care."

We also began publishing translations of books by other

Black writers. Our first translation was *Black Power: Politics of Liberation in America,* by Kwame Ture and Charles Hamilton, with a foreword by Bokar Ture, Kwame's son. As I write this, in 2023, we are preparing to translate women authors of the Global South into Portuguese. We will be publishing the Black Colombian writer Velia Vidal, as well as the book *Dalit Feminism,* written by various Dalit researchers, both men and women. All in all, through the Sueli Carneiro imprint, the Plural Feminisms Collection, and our other enterprises combined, we have sold over half a million books and published twenty-five volumes.

In 2018, after publishing *Lugar de fala,* I signed on with the venerated publishing house Companhia das Letras. In 2019 they published my essay collection *Who's Afraid of Black Feminism?* My next book, *A Short Antiracist Manual* (inspired by Ibram X. Kendi's *How to Be an Antiracist*), was Brazil's best-selling book of 2020, was still on best-seller lists more than a hundred weeks later, and won the Jabuti Prize, Brazil's most prestigious literary award. In 2021 came the publication of my most recent book, *Letters to My Grandmother,* a personal memoir in letters to my late maternal grandmother, Antonia; in 2022 *Transatlantic Dialogues,* a collection of conversations between myself and Nadia Yala, a professor of philosophy at the University of Paris 8, appeared. My books can be found in classrooms throughout Brazil; they are read and discussed in schools and in college courses.

It's been a long road to get here as a Black Brazilian woman. *Lugar de fala* has appeared in French, Italian, Spanish, and German. *Who's Afraid of Black Feminism?* has French and Spanish editions; *A Short Antiracist Manual* has come out in French, Italian, and Spanish, and *Letters to My Grand-*

mother in Spanish and Italian. But the internationalization of my publishing project has been as important to me as my own books. To bring it about, I negotiated and secured translations of six books from the Plural Feminisms Collection into French and three into Italian. We have organized three promotional tours for our authors through France and Belgium for the French translations, with all expenses paid by the project. The majority of Americans and Europeans still have a stereotyped idea of Brazil and no knowledge of our intellectual production. So the internationalization of the Collection was fundamental, disseminating through translations the thinking of the Brazilian authors we have published.

As a writer, I have participated in events and book fairs in France, Italy, Germany, Belgium, Colombia, Argentina, Peru, Scotland, the United States, Mexico, and the Netherlands. I have been made a member of the São Paulo Academy of Letters. I was the first Brazilian to participate in the Edinburgh Book Fair, to give the keynote address to the United Nations General Assembly on the International Day of Remembrance of the Victims of Slavery and the Transatlantic Slave Trade, and to be honored with BET's International Global Good Award. In 2019 I was honored with a Prince Claus Award, bestowed by the Dutch government to "honor individuals and organizations reflecting a progressive and contemporary approach to the themes of culture and development," and in 2023 I was awarded the Franco-German Prize for Human Rights and the Rule of Law. All these awards were in recognition of my work to democratize knowledge and transform the publishing market in Brazil.

And our project has yielded massive results. The number of Black authors published in Brazil by other publishers has grown exponentially. Beyond all these prizes, the greatest reward has come from the people's strength—seeing Black writers read and studied in schools, receiving letters from students all over the country who see themselves in our books, witnessing many more Black authors receiving prizes. As Glauber Rocha's character Corisco famously shouted with his dying breath in *Black God, White Devil*, "The people will win out."

One of my greatest joys was playing a role in the Brazilian reissues of Toni Morrison's books. In 2019 I was invited to curate a book subscription club, and I nominated my favorite book, *The Bluest Eye*. At the time, Toni Morrison's work was out of print in Brazil since she had long been considered a "hard-to-read author." After my selection, the subscription club sold forty thousand copies, which led to an increased interest in Morrison's books, prompting the rightsholder to reissue them. Morrison's agent approached me about writing a foreword for the subscription club edition, and so I had the honor of providing that for the Brazilian edition of the book that changed my life.

None of this has been easy. Brazilian Portuguese writers do not typically have access to an international readership. As a Black Brazilian author who dared to question the norms of the Brazilian publishing marketplace, I've been on the receiving end of many attacks, and many people have attempted to stop my work. I know I'm a woman who challenges centers of power—and I think it is important to be that way. Comfort doesn't bring about change. It's for precisely this reason that I'm thrilled to see *Where We Stand*—a book that explains "speaking place," an important concept in Brazil that does not yet exist in English—brought out in America by such an established and respected publisher. We need to show readers a different Brazil—a powerful one that transforms, fights, and transcends.

We once received an offer from a prestigious American publisher to translate a book from the Collection. The proposal was for a book written by a man (yes, Plural Feminisms mostly publishes Black women, but we also publish works by Black men). We met with the publisher and presented our other books, written by women. The editor responded, "We never even publish works by the greatest African *American* feminist philosophers," leaving unsaid the coda "much less a Black Brazilian woman." Following this xenophobic and sexist answer, we cut the conversation short. The moment had not yet arrived for a literary project by a Black Brazilian woman who takes pride in her roots.

I finished college at thirty-two, defended my master's thesis at thirty-five, published the original Brazilian edition of *Where We Stand* at thirty-seven, wrote *Letters to My Grandmother* at forty, and now, at almost forty-three, I'm seeing the first English translation of one of my books. Those who hurry have always seen me as a slowpoke. In the mythology of the *orixás,* the candomblé deities, I am a daughter of Oxóssi, the hunter with a single arrow. Precisely because he has only one arrow, he is accurate. He hunts alone but always for his community.

There's a story about Oxóssi that says the hunter doesn't hurry. Hurrying means running the risk of missing the mark. Today, seeing how far we've come, the ways our community has been nourished by Black literature and Black thought, I see that time was always on our side. May this book nourish dreams, enrich the repertoires of those still unaware of Black Brazilian feminist writing, and open up new possibilities for being and thinking to a new world.

1

A Brief History Lesson

> The risk we take here is in the act of speaking out, with
> all its implications. It's precisely because we have been
> spoken of, infantilized (infants: those who don't have
> speech of their own, who speak of themselves in the
> third person, because they are spoken of by adults), that
> in this work we take on our own voice. Which is to say,
> the trash will speak, and we don't care what you think.
>
> —Lélia Gonzalez, "Racism and Sexism in Brazilian
> Culture"

I am part of a long tradition. For centuries, Black women
have fought for recognition as political subjects, while also
generating arguments against prevailing hierarchies. Barred
from and ignored by the brokers of institutional and political power, we have been forced to devise creative strategies
to raise our voices. I want to begin by tracing the intellectual
roadmaps and battle strategies of Black women, beginning
with an example of how a Black woman I admire spoke into
the concentrated centers of power nearly two centuries ago.

Born into captivity in Swartekill, New York, Isabella Baum-
free assumed the name Sojourner Truth in 1843 and became

an abolitionist, orator, and women's rights activist. At the 1851 Ohio Woman's Rights Convention in Akron, she delivered her famous speech, widely known as "Ain't I a Woman?" A printed version of this improvised speech was popularized some twelve years later by Frances Gage, a feminist and coauthor of a huge compendium of materials on first-wave feminism, *History of Woman Suffrage*. The first recorded version of the speech, however, was published by Marcus Robinson, in the June 21, 1851, edition of *The Anti-Slavery Bugle,* and it probably did not contain the famous titular words. Instead of a question—*Ain't I a woman?*—we have a declaration: *I, a Black woman, am a woman's rights.*[1]

> May I say a few words? . . . I want to say a few words about this matter. I am a woman's rights. I have as much muscle as any man, and can do as much work as any man. I have plowed and reaped and husked and chopped and mowed, and can any man do more than that? I have heard much about the sexes being equal; I can carry as much as any man, and can eat as much too, if I can get it. I am as strong as any man that is now. . . . The Lady has spoken about Jesus, how he never spurned woman from him, and she was right. When Lazarus died, Mary and Martha came to him with faith and love and besought him to raise their brother. And Jesus wept—and Lazarus came forth. And how came Jesus into the world? Through God who created him and woman who bore him. Man, where is your part? But the women are coming up blessed be God and a few of the men are coming up with them. But man is in a tight place, the poor slave is on him, woman is coming on him, and he is surely between a hawk and a buzzard.[2]

As early as the nineteenth century, Sojourner Truth's speech exposed a major dilemma that mainstream feminism would have to confront: the universalized category of "woman." When Sojourner Truth says, *"I am a woman's rights,"* she is asserting that Black women occupy a vital place in the women's rights movement. Today, thanks to third-wave feminism, we are able to move beyond the structural universal when talking about women, and take into account factors such as race, sexual orientation, and gender identity.[3] But Sojourner Truth's speech, along with Black women's forgotten histories of resistance, intellectual legacies since before slavocracy, and political and social activism, testifies to the reality that this battle was already well under way long ago. The problem was its invisibility to the eyes of the powerful—particularly those within the feminist movement.

As we can see from Sojourner Truth, regardless of whether you consider her a feminist in the usual sense of that term, awareness of intersecting identities within feminism was present from the first wave of feminism—and before. Furthermore, the works of thinkers such as bell hooks and Audre Lorde, among others, show that it persisted through the second wave. Though Truth probably never uttered the question, *Ain't I a woman?* became a rallying cry for generations of Black feminists, including hooks, whose 1981 book by this title is a foundational work, one of the first to highlight the intersecting identities present within feminism. Yet throughout both the first and the second wave of feminism, discussions of intersectionality were largely relegated to the sidelines, considered marginal to more central topics such as voting rights and women's status in the workplace.[4]

Giovana Xavier, a professor at the Federal University of

Rio de Janeiro (UFRJ) and an organizer of the study group and directory Visible Black Intellectuals, seeks to center Black feminist advocacy, restoring it to its rightful place as an integral part of feminist history. In her article "Feminism: Copyright of a Beautiful Black Practice," she asserts:

> In this dialogue, which is also about protagonism, listening ability, and speaking place, we ask these questions: Which stories are untold? Who, in Brazil and in the world, are the trailblazers initiating social projects and conducting experiments in the name of equality and liberty? Whose voice was suppressed for a single story of feminism to become the truth? . . . As guardians of this ancestral heritage, it is on us to bring visibility to these histories of glory and creativity we carry. This turning point in our narratives connects to the primary agenda of Black feminism: the act of restoring denied humanities.[5]

Nearly two hundred years ago, Sojourner Truth challenged the dominant conceptualization of feminism, asserted herself as a protagonist, and in so doing sought to restore such denied humanities. In another speech, called "On Woman's Dress," she declares,

> When I saw them women on the stage at the Woman's Suffrage Convention the other day I thought, What kind of reformers be you, with goose wings on your heads, as if you were going to fly, and dressed in such ridiculous fashion, talking about reform and women's rights? 'Pears to me you had better reform yourselves first. But Sojourner is an old body, and will soon get out of this world into

another, and wants to say when she gets there, Lord, I
have done my duty, I have told the whole truth and kept
nothing back.[6]

In mocking the goose-feather hat, Sojourner Truth emphasizes that she is speaking about the women of privilege who were on the front lines of the women's suffrage
movement. When she says, "you had better reform your-
selves first," she indicts their failure to recognize the experiences of Black women and to see the perpetuation of racism as relevant to the feminist agenda. What mattered to
white women was gaining rights for themselves, a priority that has endured even as Black women write and speak
about their ongoing lack of recognition as a political category. Sojourner Truth's words remind us that voices forgotten by mainstream feminism have been speaking for a long
time. The question that follows is this: Why has it taken so
long for them to be heard?[7]

The activist's voice pierces and disrupts the dominant
history of feminism; it peals with the urgency of its existence. It testifies that throughout history, Black women have
rebelled against the dominant model, have challenged its
narratives. With all this in mind, if we are to do away with
outdated notions of what feminism is, we must start from
scratch to build something that can house all of us.

The Black feminist thinker Lélia Gonzalez, who critiqued
the hierarchization of knowledge as a result of racial classi-
fications, provides valuable insights toward formulating an
inclusive feminism. She draws our attention to this essential
equation: whoever possesses social privilege possesses epistemic privilege, since the recognized universal model of sci-

ence is white. This hierarchy confers superiority on Euro-centric epistemology, legitimating modern Western thought exclusively as valid knowledge, giving it structural dominance, and thus dismissing as invalid other ways of knowing. According to Gonzalez, racism was built on "the 'science' of Euro-Christian (white and patriarchal) superiority."[8] Her reflections give us clues as to who can speak and who cannot—which voices are deemed credible, and which are not.

Gonzalez also reflects on the absence of Black and Indigenous voices in mainstream feminism, critiquing the exclusive reproduction by intellectuals and activists of a white European feminism, which fails to give due importance to the realities experienced by women of color, particularly in colonized countries. For Gonzalez, analyses based solely on patriarchal capitalism are not fully applicable to Black and Indigenous women in Latin America because another type of discrimination, as serious as the others already mentioned, is absent from the equations: racial oppression.

She discusses these women's various trajectories and resistance strategies, and upholds a Black Latin American feminism, offering as evidence the legacy of struggle, those shared, well-worn paths toward confronting racism and sexism. Which is to say, more than sharing experiences based in slavery, racism, or colonialism, what these women have in common is *means of resistance.*

In many of her texts, she also confronts the dominant linguistic paradigm by using a language that does not obey normative grammatical rules, giving visibility to the linguistic legacy of formerly enslaved persons.[9] In this way, her writing actively works to decolonize knowledge and refute epistemological neutrality. It is fundamental for many Black and

Latina feminists to address the ways the dominant language is wielded to maintain power, by excluding those who have been cut off from the sorts of opportunities granted by a fair system of education. Beyond being an impediment to more transgressive, radical forms of education, language can be a barrier to understanding, and can encourage the creation of more compartmentalized spaces of power.[10] Gonzalez reflects on the way people who speak "wrong," according to what we understand to be "proper" or "the norm," are treated with disdain and condescension. She valorizes the language of Black African peoples enslaved in Brazil, calling it *pretuguês* or "blaccent."

> It's funny how they (elitist white society) make fun of us
> when we say we're "Framengo" fans. They call us ignorant,
> saying that we talk wrong. Maybe they don't realize
> that using an /r/ in place of an /l/ is nothing more than
> a linguistic feature of an African language, in which /l/
> doesn't exist. In the end, who's the ignoramus? At the same
> time, they think that "Brazilian" speech—cutting r's off of
> infinitives, condensing you-all into y'all, it is to it's, and so
> on and so forth—is where it's at. They don't get that they're
> speaking with a blaccent.[11]

Much as Gonzalez challenges the dominant epistemology, so does the Panamanian-American philosopher Linda Alcoff. In "An Epistemology for the Next Revolution," Alcoff critiques the imposition of a universal epistemology that disregards "the knowledge claims of midwives, the ontologies of First Nations peoples, the medical practices of the colonized, and even first-person experiential reports of ev-

ery sort," and which confers legitimacy on itself as "the pro-
tocol theory for discursive mastery." As she puts it:

> Is it realistic to believe that a single "master epistemology"
> can judge every kind of knowledge claim from every
> cultural and social location? Universal knowledge
> claims about knowledge itself need, at minimum, a deep
> reflexivity about their own cultural and social location.[12]

Alcoff elucidates the need to take into account other ways
of knowing. Within the Brazilian context, this could include
the knowledge of candomblé priestesses, the Ialorixás and
Babalorixás, the women in the movement fighting for child-
care, community leaders, Black sisterhoods, social movements, cosmogonies of African-derived religions, and other
geographies of reason and knowledge. It is necessary, then,
if we are to transcend implied discursive authorization, to
question and challenge the way identities have been constructed in these contexts. Here, bell hooks shows us the way.

In "Black Women Intellectuals," she explores how, within
a racist paradigm, Black women are primarily understood
with reference to the body instead of ideas. She asserts that
racism and sexism in combination have led the narrow-
minded to see us as outsiders in the intellectual realm. Furthermore, the very conception of what the paradigmatic
intellectual is—white and Western—makes this path more
difficult for Black women to take. Crossing this boundary,
bell hooks defines herself as an intellectual, but one who
unites theory and practice to understand her concrete reality.
Theory and practice, here, are not bifurcated but rather are
dialectical, in conversation with each other.[13]

It is common for Black feminists such as hooks to be accused of "playing the race card" or focusing too much on identity politics. In online discussions, we often see comments like "activists would rather discuss identity politics than confront the challenges of class." Alcoff offers us a valuable way to think about why identity is necessarily relevant to political reality. In order to decolonize knowledge, she argues, we need to recognize social identity—not only in order to demonstrate how colonization has created those very identities but also to show how certain identities have historically been silenced and epistemically delegitimized while others have been privileged. Along these lines, decolonizing knowledge necessarily requires thinking about the importance of identity, since it reflects the fact that experiences vary by location and that, as Alcoff puts it, "location is important for knowledge":

> This will open us up to charges once again that we are falling into identity politics, that we are metaphysically unsophisticated and politically retrograde, a critique that has too often been wielded from the metropole to the peripheries in the global academy. The critiques of identity politics have held too many in thrall to the charge of crass political essentialism and lack of theoretical sophistication. I believe that the anti-identity trend so prevalent in social theory today is another stumbling block to the very project of decolonizing knowledge, since it undermines our ability to articulate what is wrong with the theoretical hegemony of the global north.

Moreover, many people involved in social justice movements have come to accept the idea that identity politics is a diversion from class struggle. Identity-based political movements are by definition class-inclusive, but more than that they are seen as divisive of a class-based agenda, as fetishizing identities, and as presenting identities in an essentialist and de-historicized way that obscures the fact that identities are the product of history and capable of dynamic change. Such critics of identity come from the right, from liberals, and from the left, and unite in their claim that identity politics fractures the body politic; that it emphasizes difference at the expense of commonalities; and that its focus on identity offers only a reductivist politics, one that would reduce or replace an assessment of a person's political view with an assessment of their identity. . . .

The problem leftists have with identity politics, however, is not just about the process of getting to the revolution, but also about what we think we are struggling for. That is, some imagine that the new imaginary communities to come will have much less emphasis on racial and ethnic differences, differences which they see as the product entirely or almost entirely of structures of oppression such as slavery and colonialism. Colonialism creates and reifies identities as ways of managing peoples and setting up hierarchies between groups. Therefore many believe we must aim for a future in which the identities created by colonialism can wither away.[14]

Alcoff's rich, complex reflection is convincing: we need to recognize how colonialism imposes identity. It is impossible to have wide-ranging discussions on a societal project without confronting how certain identities are molded within colonial logic.

In any discussion of identity, our objective in confronting the norm is not merely to talk about identity but to unveil the ways that institutions *use* identity to oppress or to privilege. What we fundamentally hope emerges from this debate is an understanding of how power and identities *work together,* depending on context, and how colonialism not only creates but delegitimizes certain identities and legitimizes others. In this way, to discuss identity is not to reduce the whole of politics to race and gender; it is rather to pay attention to the fact that inequalities are created by the way power articulates certain identities. Identities emerge out of a structure of oppression that privileges certain groups to the detriment of others, and to ignore this is to fail to understand how political systems function.

Very often, white people insist on not perceiving their own identifiers. In light of the ways identities were forged in colonial societies, for example, this means that they can go on saying that only they think of the collective whole, and that Black people, in reclaiming their ways of being, their politics and intellectual lives, are being separatist and only thinking of themselves. By persisting in the belief that their experience is universal and that they speak for everyone, white people insist on speaking for others when, in fact, they are speaking only on their own behalf. Yet they persist in thinking that what they say is universally applicable.

Thus, we come to understand why Black feminists think of Black women as a political category. These reflections will help us understand the concept of a *speaking place,* to which we now turn.

2

The Black Woman

I am not going away; *I* am going to stay here and *stand the fire!*

—Sojourner Truth

One of the core tenets of Black feminism is that Black women's stories and experiences matter and should be shared. This may seem so self-evident that it goes without saying, but as we have seen from the history of publishing in Brazil, the assumption is that our experiences and our stories in fact do *not* matter and are *not* worth sharing. We face the double bind of the colonial gaze and the male gaze directed onto our bodies, our knowledge, and our production, and, more than simply refuting that gaze, we ultimately need a different starting point. Speaking about our experiences allows us to define ourselves outside the legacy of the colonizers—to tell a different story about who we are, to inhabit an alternative narrative. Who have others considered us to be, and who do *we* say we are?

It has been said that woman is not thought of on her own

terms but in relation to man, in opposition—as the other of man, or that which is not man. The French philosopher Simone de Beauvoir coined this feminist understanding of the *Other* in *The Second Sex,* taking as her starting point G. W. F. Hegel's dialectic of master and slave.

According to Beauvoir's diagnosis, men relate to women in terms of domination and submission, since women are entangled in the bad faith of men who see and desire them as objects, rather than as subjects.[1] In her philosophical exploration of gender, Beauvoir posits that women are defined by the male gaze instead of on their own terms. It is this gaze that confines them to a submissive role in the social hierarchy.

Beauvoir argues that this category of the Other is so ancient and widespread that, according to her investigations, a duality was already present in the oldest mythologies and primitive societies: that of *Same* versus *Other.* This division would initially have been established not on the basis of sex but rather because otherness was a fundamental category of human thought. "No group ever self-defines as the *One* without immediately putting the *Other* opposite itself," says Beauvoir:

> For villagers, all those who do not belong to the village are suspect "others"; for those born in a country, the inhabitants of another country are seen as "foreigners"; Jews are "others" for the anti-Semite, as are Blacks for American racists, Indigenes for the colonists, proletarians for the privileged classes. At the end of a deep study of the various forms of primitive societies, Lévi-Strauss

was able to conclude, "Passage from the state of Nature to the state of Culture is defined by man's ability to view biological relations as a series of oppositions: duality, alternation, opposition, and symmetry, whether these present in definite or less clear forms, are not phenomena to be explained so much as fundamental and immediate givens of social reality." These phenomena would be incomprehensible if human society were strictly a *Mitsein*, or fellowship, based on solidarity and friendliness. On the contrary, they become clear if, following Hegel, we find in consciousness itself a fundamental hostility toward every other consciousness; the subject only ever positions itself in opposition—it stakes a claim as the essential, and sets the other up as the inessential, the object.[2]

For Beauvoir, "woman" was constituted as the Other since she was seen as an object, in the interpretation the French philosopher made using the Sartrean concept "in-itself." Simply put, this means thinking of "woman" as a thing with a function. A chair, for example, is useful because it lets people sit; a pen is useful because it allows us to write.

Thinking of people in this way is fundamentally dehumanizing. But the masculine gaze, according to Beauvoir, conceptualizes woman as object, preventing her from being "for-herself"—a subject, in Sartre's ontological parlance. And this also explains why the world, with all its possibilities, is not open to women. A woman's place is the place of the Other.

If for Simone de Beauvoir woman is the Other in not being able to reciprocate the male gaze, the Portuguese artist and writer Grada Kilomba argues that the Black woman is the *Other of the Other,* put in a position where reciprocity is even more complicated:

> Black women have thus been positioned within several discourses that misrepresent our own reality: a debate on race where the subject is Black male; a gendered discourse where the subject is *white* female; and a discourse on class where "race" has no place at all. We occupy a very critical place within theory.
>
> It is because of this ideological lack, argues Heidi Safia Mirza (1997) that Black women inhabit an empty space, a space that overlaps the margins of "race" and gender, the so-called "third space." We inhabit a kind of vacuum of erasure and contradiction "sustained by the polarization of the world into Blacks on one side and women on the other." . . . Us in between. This is, of course, a serious theoretical dilemma, in which the concepts of "race" and gender narrowly merge into one. Such separate narratives maintain the invisibility of Black women in academic and political debates.[3]

For Kilomba, it is necessary to confront this lack of recognition. She complicates our perception of the category of the Other by asserting that Black women, in being neither white nor men, occupy a very difficult place in white supremacist society: a kind of double deficit, the antithesis both of whiteness and of masculinity. From this point of view, she perceives the status of white women as variable, since they are women, but white; she makes a related and similar assessment of Black men's status, since they are

Black, but men. Black women, within this analytic frame, being neither white nor men, are the Other of the Other.[4]

We can see here the ways that Kilomba takes Beauvoir's schema and expands upon it. For the French philosopher, there is no possible reciprocity between women and men since the woman is always regarded through the male gaze as subordinate, the absolute Other. But Beauvoir's assertion refers to a specific way of being a woman, which is to say, a white woman. Kilomba adds another dimension by advancing the case that, as the Other of the Other, the Black woman is never permitted to be herself, whereas a variable status permits both white women and Black men potentially to emplace themselves as subjects.

Beyond demonstrating that women experience varying levels of otherness, Kilomba also breaks with universality with regard to men, showing that the reality of Black men is not the same as that of white men. As she demonstrates, we need to ask which men we are talking about.[5]

It is critically important to recognize the victimization of Black men by racism, which places them beneath white women in the social pyramid. Calling attention to these identities is an urgent priority, and Kilomba does so by universalizing neither the category of woman nor that of man. Recognizing vacillation in the statuses of both white women and Black men makes it possible for us to discern these groups' specific lived realities and to pierce the fog of invisibility surrounding the experiences of Black women.

To offer a concrete example: it is still very common to hear the following assertion in discussions of salary inequality: "Women earn 20 percent less than men in Brazil." Is this statement incorrect? Technically no, but it offers an inaccurate picture and obscures social realities. In 2022 in the state of São Paulo, while women as a whole earned 20 percent less than men, Black women earned approximately 50 percent less than white men. This metric also fails to take into account the fact that Black women in Brazil have a much higher rate of precarious employment (temporary, poorly paid, and without legal protections) than any other group, and are the largest contingent among the unemployed and those in domestic labor. Similarly, in the United States in 2022, according to the Pew Research Center, on average, women earned 18 percent less than men. But if we break this figure down by race, we see that Black women earned 35 percent less than White men.[6]

This metric, which specifies both race and gender, along with other reports that take into account the status of various social groups, gets closest to representing reality—and thereby generates demand for changes in public policies. Insisting on a homogenous vision of men and women keeps the lived realities of Black men and Black women invisible, such that they not only fail to benefit from important policies but move ever farther from the centers of power where such policies are determined.

There is a growing emphasis on the importance of public policies benefiting women, and we frequently hear that women's rights are human rights—that these policies are for everyone's benefit. But who is "everyone"? Women may be vulnerable, but Black women are the most vulnerable among them, specifically because our society produces certain inequalities; the failure to take a close look at their condition makes truly meaningful progress impossible. We have to understand that to improve the human development index of vulnerable groups is to improve the human development index of a city, a country. To do this, it is necessary to focus on that reality—or, as Black feminists have been asserting forever, to *name* it. If a reality is not named, it remains invisible, and there will be no thought of improving it. Insistence on talking about women in universal terms, without taking note of their distinct experiences, means that vulnerable women are only partly visible. According to the 2015 *Violence Map* of Brazil, murders of Black women increased by 54.8 percent in the same period that murders of white women decreased by 9.6 percent.[7] This alarming increase shows us the lack of ethnic-racial considerations in the conception of policies intended to confront violence against women, since these policies are not helping Black women. The majority of "women" being helped by these public policies are white.

To further elucidate this argument, we present data from an important study that made visible a violent reality that affected and, unfortunately, still affects Black women in Brazil. In the 1980s, Black women were forcibly sterilized. According to research by the physician and human rights activist Jurema Werneck, the Black Women's Movement has been at the helm of efforts to combat this genocide of the Black population and erosion of women's liberty, beginning with a denunciation of the practice.[8] Their actions resulted in the creation of a Parliamentary Commission of Inquiry in 1991. The Sterilization Inquiry, as it has come to be known, verified that the practice was ongoing, whether owing to inadequate contraceptive education and options offered by privately funded institutions, primarily in the poorest regions of the country, or simply as an irreversible contraceptive measure. If Black women had not spoken out against this practice and fought to bring its violence into the open, the situation would probably be graver still.

Bringing these cases to light and analyzing them from all the relevant perspectives (Black, female, Brazilian) under an intersectional lens shows us how crucial it is to leave behind simplistic analyses, to resist the temptation of a universality that excludes. History has shown us that invisibility kills, that which the philosopher Michel Foucault calls "to make live or let die," which is to say that you can't fight what you don't name. If we ignore oppressed groups' reality, we effectively kill them by neglect. The takeaway here is the recognition that when Black folk reclaim the right to a voice, they reclaim the right to their own lives.

In *The Second Sex,* Beauvoir argues that when individuals are kept in an inferior position, they *are* de facto inferiors. For Beauvoir, the key to this formulation is understanding "being" in the dynamic, Hegelian sense. That is, she says, "being"—or to be—"is to have become, to have been made as one manifests. Yes, women, as a whole, *are,* today, inferior to men; which is to say, their situation offers them lesser possibilities."[9]

Black women are in a situation in which the concrete material possibilities are lesser still, and this being so, nothing is more ethical than to find emancipatory exits from this predicament of social and political exclusion—that is, to fight for a voice, for better conditions. In this sense, we urgently need to displace hegemonic thinking and redefine identities, whether of race, gender, or class, in order to amplify the voice and visibility of those who have been rendered invisible by the mainstream "norm."[10]

In short, Kilomba argues that being the antithesis of both whiteness and masculinity makes it difficult for Black women to be seen as subjects. The white and Black male gazes, along with that of white women, confines Black women to an inferior position that is tough to transcend. The American scholar and professor Patricia Hill Collins offers us another interesting insight into the place of the Other and the necessity for Black women to define themselves:

> Black women's insistence on self-definition, self-valuation, and the necessity for a Black female-centered analysis is significant for two reasons. First, defining and valuing one's consciousness of one's own self-defined standpoint in the face of images that foster a self-definition as the objectified "other" is an important way of resisting the dehumanization essential to systems of domination. The status of being the "other" implies being "other than" or different from the assumed norm of white male behavior. In this model, powerful white males define themselves as subjects, the true actors, and classify people of color and women in terms of their position vis-à-vis the male hub. Since Black women have been denied the authority to challenge these definitions, this model consists of images that define Black women as a negative other, the virtual antithesis of positive white male images.

Clearly, self-definition is a crucial step toward empowerment and toward identifying possible ways to transcend the colonizing norm. In her article "Learning from the Outsider Within: The Sociological Significance of Black Feminist Thought," Collins speaks of the importance of Black women

making creative use of the marginal place they occupy in society toward developing theories and thinking that reflect diverse views and perspectives.[11]

The concept of the "outsider within" is very important
to our subsequent understanding of the concept of *speaking
place*. For Collins, Black women within the feminist movement occupy the place of the "outsider within": they are
feminists staking a claim for Black women as political subjects—the exact right for which white women fought in first-
wave feminism—but they are seen and treated as outsiders
within the heart of the feminist movement.

Collins understands the predicament of the *outsider
within* as a social position or border space occupied by different groups with unequal power. In academia, for example, this place allows Black women researchers, working
from their own experiences, to attest to anomalies most often manifested in the omission or distortion of certain social facts. Although Collins is speaking of sociology, it is possible to think of this as a political practice applicable across
any and all academic fields. Collins further argues that Black
women, even while forming part of various institutions, are
not thought of as equals. She gives the examples of domestic
workers employed in homes: white people will indicate such
employees' importance by saying they are "practically family," even while they continue to occupy a marginal place.[12]

"On one level," says Collins, "this 'insider' relationship
has been satisfying to all involved. The memoirs of afflu-
ent whites often mention their love for their Black 'mothers,'
while accounts of Black domestic workers stress the sense of
self-affirmation they experienced at seeing white power de-
mystified—of knowing that it was not the intellect, talent or

humanity of their employers that supported their superior status, but largely just the advantages of racism."[13]

Collins points out, however, that we must learn to take advantage of our outsider position, since this space allots Black women a specific vantage point, one that grants them a view of a wider spectrum of society. Unsurprisingly, in their thinking about concepts such as intersectionality and revolution, these women set out not only to consider structural oppression in isolation but to conceive of new forms of social life. It is as if Black women occupied a non-place, but, further, as if they perceive the pain of this non-place while being equally aware of it as a place of potential.

Sueli Carneiro gives us yet another way to understand Black women's subjectivity:

When we speak of the myth of feminine fragility, which historically justified men's paternalistic protection over women, which women are we speaking of? We, Black women, form part of a contingent of women, probably the majority, who never recognized ourselves in this myth, because we have never been treated as fragile. We form part of a contingent of women who have worked for centuries as slaves in the fields or on the streets, selling snacks, selling fruits and vegetables, selling our bodies. . . . We are women who don't understand when feminists say women need to take to the streets and work. We form part of a contingent of women identified as objects. . . .

We originate in a culture that has been violated, folklorized, and marginalized, treated like a primitive thing, a thing of the devil, something else that's alien to our culture. We form part of a contingent of women whose specifics are ignored by the medical system, because the myth of racial democracy that we've all internalized makes it unnecessary to note patients' skin color on the public health system's forms, information that would be indispensable for evaluating the health condition of Black women in Brazil, since we know, from other countries' data, that white and Black women have significant differences in terms of health.

Therefore, we need a feminist perspective in which gender is a theoretical variable, but, as Linda Alcoff and fellow feminist scholar Elizabeth Potter state, gender can't be considered "separable from other axes of oppression and susceptible to a unique analysis. . . . If feminism is to liberate women, it must address virtually all forms of domination." From this point of view, it is possible to assert that a Black feminism, constructed in the context of multiracial, multicultural and racist societies—as is the case for Latin American societies—has racism and its impact on gender relations as its primary axis of articulation, since this determines the hierarchy of gender itself within our societies.[14]

Carneiro shows us that racism determines gender hierarchies in our society, which is why it is necessary for feminist movements to come up with ways to fight this oppression. If they do not, they help to maintain hierarchical relationships among women, and thus reproduce existing power structures. What's more, Carneiro's analysis reveals why it is necessary for Black women to reclaim their identity and define themselves as political and historical subjects. It is fundamental, however, that we pay attention to this category's surrounding heterogeneities, so that we do not think of it as fixed or stable.

One notable characteristic of many Black feminists is that they do not conceive of themselves solely as theoreticians but also define themselves as activists, even militants. Black feminism, according to writer and theorist Ana Angélica Sebastião, is a political, intellectual, and theory-making movement of Black women involved in the fight against inequality to promote real social change. These women are not concerned only with identifying the oppressions that affect them; they are actively searching for solutions. Black women are discussing and debating social remedies.[15]

The work of Audre Lorde, a Black-Caribbean lesbian feminist, further amplifies the call to engage with difference around identity. In many of her writings, Lorde stressed the importance of not hierarchizing oppressions, and her own struggle to feel as though she belonged to any movement, given that the feminist movement prioritized gender, the Black movement race, and the LGBTQ+ movement sexual orientation. As a Black woman and a lesbian, she felt forced to choose which oppression to fight, with each separate identity assigning her a place. Lorde said she could never deny one identity to embrace another, since doing that would lead not to real transformation but to mere reformism, just as Sojourner Truth had implied a century earlier. In response, Lorde emphasized the importance of widening our lens, and urged us to pose this question: To what degree do we legitimate the power we condemn?

In her 1979 speech at New York University "The Master's Tools Will Never Dismantle the Master's House," Lorde calls on us to consider intersectionality, saying that white women need to take responsibility for combating reformism and "recognize difference as a crucial strength." In a 1980 essay "Age, Race, Class, and Sex," she says, "The true focus of revolutionary change is never merely the oppressive situations we seek to escape, but that piece of the oppressor which is planted deep within each of us." [16]

The problem is that differences often signify inequalities. Failing to recognize that we have different starting places and that we experience gender differently effectively legitimizes an exclusionary discourse by failing to make visible various ways of being a woman in the world. This attention to what Lorde calls the evasion of responsibility by white women, in not committing to change, can be understood as a failure of ethical understanding: thinking of the world only from one's own social locus. The fact that white women do not demarcate these places, and subsequently ignore that different women have different starting points, allows them to continue ignoring the task of questioning themselves, and, consequently, to continue reproducing oppressions against Black women or against, as Lorde calls them, "those who stand outside the circle of this society's definition of acceptable women"—those who, from their social places, know that *survival is not an academic skill.*"[17]

So far, so good? If so, let's dive deeper into what a *speaking place* might be.

3
What Is a Speaking Place?

Why do I write? Cause I have to. Cause my voice, in all its dialects, has been silenced too long.

—Suheir Hammad

All the lines of reasoning we have traced up to this point have been necessary in order to lay the foundation for our understanding of the term "speaking place." But before going farther, it is important to clarify that when we use the word "discourse" throughout this book, and discuss the importance of disrupting the regime of discursive authorization, we are referring to Foucault's definition.[1] That is, we are not thinking of a discourse as a pile of words or a chain of sentences with a claim to meaning in themselves but rather as a system that structures a specific social imaginary. We are talking about how words organize power and control.

All those involved in social movements are probably familiar with the debates surrounding the idea that sometimes those with power should step back and refrain from voicing their ideas, sometimes even those with power within the same movements, working toward the same ends. In no sense do I want to diminish the militancy generated by the virtual world, and of course, social movements require social cohesion and collaboration. However, it is crucial to understand that oftentimes important concepts and ideas (such as *speaking place*) can be emptied of their complexity and capacity—cheapened and reduced—because groups that have always held power are discomfited by the advance of a discourse on rights by minority groups. Before we explore what writers such as Grada Kilomba, Patricia Hill Collins, Linda Alcoff, and the feminist theorist Gayatri Spivak have to say about this, let us examine this concept from other perspectives, to offer a fuller picture.

Speaking place is a dynamic concept that operates at the nexus of a variety of disciplines, including communications studies, gender studies, race studies, and more. In communications studies, for example, speaking place has been described by Márcia Franz Amaral as a "theoretical-methodological instrument that creates an explanatory environment to demonstrate that popular and academic publications speak from different places and give various spaces to various sources and readers."[2] When applied to journalism, the concept requires us to examine inherited assumptions about credibility, power, and audience.

Furthermore, in this example, speaking place "recognizes the implications of both publications' and readers' symbolic social positions and incorporates the notion of a marketplace of readers, based on the idea that to explain any discourse, it is necessary to know the group within which it operates and the conditions of that group's formation." Put simply, in communications studies, this concept could serve to explore and analyze the differences between the speaking place of the popular press and the speaking place of an academic journal. Amaral's article, specifically, shows that the popular press's place goes beyond sensationalism and can be a rigorous form of truth-seeking, born of a deep understanding of social and political realities. For its writer, it is necessary to understand social positions and symbolic capital as distinct:

> Instead of sensationalism, a label that indicates the intensity of sensations generated by strategies such as inventions, exaggerations, distortions, and omissions, the speaking place seeks to explain why the press aimed at this audience operates with modes of address distinct from those used in reference publications, and builds credibility in other ways. To our way of seeing, the speaking place of the mainstream press is different from that of the reference journals.[3]

Here we see the attempt to analyze various discourses in light of different groups' social locations. Moreover, given the conditions under which a group was constructed and in which a given discourse operates, there might be a break with the dominant vision and an attempt to characterize the speaking place of the popular press in new ways. It is interesting to note the similarities with our focus here on Black feminism.

We should stress that the term "speaking place" has no fixed epistemology specific to it. Or perhaps it would be better to say that the term's origins (in Portuguese) are unclear. We believe that it emerges out of the traditions of feminist standpoint theory, critical race theory, and postcolonial theory. The reflections and works generated by those perspectives, subsequently, have been shaped within social movements, particularly virtual debate, into a political tool, and as a stand against discursive authorization. We affirm that one of the objectives of Black feminism is demarcating the speaking place of the speaker; moreover, we assert that this demarcation has become *necessary* for understanding realities formerly taken as implicit within the mainstream "norm."

There are scholars who consider speaking place in relation to psychoanalysis, to works by Michel Foucault or by Linda Alcoff and Gayatri Spivak, such as "An Epistemology for the Next Revolution," and *Can the Subaltern Speak?* In order to understand its applications in Black feminist thought, we turn to Patricia Hill Collins's conception of feminist standpoint theory and Grada Kilomba's study *Plantation Memories: Episodes of Everyday Racism,* considering their ideas as applied to the Brazilian context.

In her article "Comment on Hekman's 'Truth and Method: Feminist Standpoint Theory Revisited': Where's the Power?" Collins confronts critiques of feminist standpoint theory in ways that are germane to further thinking on speaking place. In this article, Collins rebuts the postmodern feminist Susan Hekman's assertions addressing the notion that feminist standpoint theory refers to individuals. Collins writes,

> First, the notion of a standpoint refers to historically shared, *group*-based experiences. Groups have a degree of permanence over time such that group realities transcend individual experiences. For example, African Americans as a stigmatized racial group existed long before I was born and will probably continue long after I die. While my individual experiences with institutionalized racism will

be unique, the types of opportunities and constraints that I encounter on a daily basis will resemble those confronting African Americans as a group. Arguing that Blacks as a group come into being or disappear on the basis of my participation seems narcissistic, egocentric, and archetypally postmodern. In contrast, standpoint theory places less emphasis on individual experiences within socially constructed groups than on the social conditions that construct such groups.[4]

As Collins explains, when we speak of starting points, we are not necessarily speaking of individual experiences, but about the social conditions that do or do not allow these groups to access full social and political participation—a structural debate. We are not trying to verify individual experiences but to understand how opportunities are restricted by the social place certain groups occupy.

Recognition of diverse experiences disrupts a universal vision. A Black woman will have experiences that are distinct from a white woman's, owing to her social location, and will experience gender differently.

According to Collins, feminist standpoint theory needs to be discussed in terms of a group's locale within power relations. It is necessary to understand the categories of race, gender, class, and sexuality as elements of the social structure that function as fundamental mechanisms contributing to inequalities and creating groups, instead of thinking of these categories as identity descriptors applied to individuals. Hekman, according to Collins's critique, understood the theory as a multitude of voices derived from individual experiences rather than as an analysis of categories causing inequalities in which these individuals find themselves. Collins uses as an example racial segregation in the United States: the way this historical fact created segregated neighborhoods and, consequently, distinct experiences in the realms of education, leisure, healthcare, and, above all, opportunities for access to certain spheres, such as academia. Collins follows up her analysis by affirming that, "moreover, middle-class Blacks have not been exempt from the effects of diminished opportunities that accompany racial segregation and group discrimination. It is common location within hierarchical power relations that creates groups, not the results of collective decision making of individuals within the groups." The approach Hekman chose—to understand groups "as an accumulation of individuals and not as entities with their own reality"—led to an erroneous critique, according to Collins.[5]

Hekman analyzes standpoint theory and speaking place from the individual perspective. This presupposition allows her to conflate individual and group as units of analysis, and so fail to realize that individuals belonging to specific groups share similar experiences. Hekman's fixation on the individual as a proxy for the group skews her understanding. Collins responds:

Initially examining only one dimension of power relations, namely, that of social class, Marx posited that, however unarticulated and inchoate, oppressed groups possessed a particular standpoint on inequality. In more contemporary versions, inequality has been revised to reflect a greater degree of complexity, especially that of race and gender. What we now have is increasing sophistication about how to discuss group location, not in the singular social class framework proposed by Marx, nor in the early feminist frameworks arguing the primacy of gender, but within constructs of multiplicity residing in social structures themselves and not in individual women.[6]

Hekman is not alone in her error. In Brazil, feminist standpoint theory is often subject to this kind of criticism, because its critics start with individuals and not with the multiple conditions creating inequalities and hierarchies within which subaltern groups are located. The experiences of these groups, socially located in dehumanized and hierarchical ways, means that their intellectual output, knowledge, and voices are equally treated as subordinate, and that social conditions keep them in a structurally silenced place. This in no way means that these groups fail to create tools to confront the institutional silences; on the contrary, they organize—politically, culturally, and intellectually. The point is that social conditions obscure and delegitimize their products and actions. A simple question to help us reflect on this: How many Black writers would college-educated readers have read or had access to during their undergraduate years? How many Black professors would they have had? How many Black journalists are there in the country's newsrooms or even in the so-called "alternative" media?

These common experiences block the Black population, occupying a defined social place, from accessing certain spheres. Thus we understand that it is possible to approach the idea of speaking place by means of feminist standpoint: the lack of access to certain spheres is tied in with the absence of those groups' intellectual products and epistemologies in those spheres; the lack of fair representation in universities, media, or electoral politics, for instance, makes it impossible for the voices of individuals in those groups to be registered or heard, even those with greater access to the internet. To speak is not merely to emit words; it is to assert one's place in the world—to assert one's right to exist, to be. In this way, the idea of speaking place refutes traditional historiography and the hierarchization of knowledge that results from social hierarchy.

When we speak of the right to a dignified existence—to a voice—we are speaking about social locus, about the way this imposed place impedes the possibility of transcendence. It has absolutely nothing to do with an essentialist idea that only Black people can talk about racism, for example.

In discussing individual group members, Collins makes clear that even if they occupy a common location with respect to hierarchical power relations, this is not to imply that they will all have the same experiences; she is not denying the individual dimension. Regardless, she indicates that, owing to shared social location, these individuals do share experiences with regard to such power relations, and it is those common experiences that she takes as objects of analysis. Collins decries the fact that critical theorists have paid excessive attention to questions of individual action rather than investigating common experiences. As an example, she cites high rates of incarceration of Black men in American prisons.

We can also draw attention to such realities in the Brazilian context: the high incidence of killings of Black women, the fact that most domestic and casual workers continue to be Black women, and countless other examples. Since these groups occupy places of greatest vulnerability, certain policies affect them most intensely. Let us look at just one particular example.

The Social Security Reform initiated in 2017 in Brazil increased contribution time to twenty-five years and the minimum age for women to begin drawing on social security from sixty to sixty-five years old. This measure did not take into consideration our societally imposed gendered division of labor. It must be said: Women are still those trained to take on domestic labor and charged with primary responsibility for childrearing. Women, particularly Black women, have different—and unequal—employment starting points, and this policy did not make provisions for or even acknowledge that reality. Various social sectors pushed back against this proposal, but the amendment became law in 2019, the only concession being that women's retirement age was only raised to sixty-two. To put it in broader context, though, Black women already had difficulty retiring long before this constitutional amendment because of their casual and irregular relationship with the labor market and, in the case of domestic workers, because they lacked labor protections. In Brazil, they have always been a marginalized group.

When Brazil formally abolished slavery—it was the last country in the Americas to do so, in 1888—it did not at the same time introduce any policy for integrating the largest contingent of Black persons outside Africa into the Brazilian social and economic fabric. As the professor of business administration Juliana Teixeira points out, this historical fact means that Black women transitioned from domestic slavery to domestic work, a reality that persists to the present day. According to 2023 data from the Brazilian Institute of

Geography and Statistics, Black women account for 65 percent of the nearly 6 million domestic workers in Brazil, and the majority work under the table for a daily or monthly wage, which means that they are not able to partake in social security benefits and are entirely unable to access the resources of the social safety net. What is more: the majority of domestic workers are over forty and earn below minimum wage.[7]

One tragic case might illustrate the dire result of the social precariousness of Black women with regard to employment. During the pandemic, many domestic workers were forced to continue working. I say "forced" because the majority were informally employed, which meant that if they did not work, they earned nothing at all, and also because, in this colonially informed cultural tradition that lies somewhere between slavery and domestic employment, employers preferred to risk their health rather than go without domestic help. Two of those domestic workers were Mirtes Renata and her mother. They worked in the same house, a high-end apartment in Recife. Mirtes, a Black woman, had a five-year-old son, Miguel Otávio. Because she had no one available to watch Miguel, Mirtes had to bring him to work with her. On June 2, 2020, Mirtes, Miguel, the employer, Sari Corte Real (the irony here: her surname means "Royal Court"), and Sari's manicurist (another informally employed Black woman) were all in the apartment. Sari told Mirtes to walk the dog. Miguel was left alone with the employer and the manicurist until Sari let him get into the elevator alone to look for his mother. Wandering the building on his own, Miguel got lost and fell nine stories. He did not survive the fall. His mother found him when she returned from walking the dog.[8]

As Juliana Teixeira has said, any one of us could be little Miguel—it is common in the Black community for children to go along with their mothers to their domestic employment. My mother was a domestic worker, just like Juliana's mother and Miguel's. The callous disregard for Black life is appalling, as is the fact that Black women such as Mirtes are shut out from the very programs that purport to be in place to assist the vulnerable. Similarly, we can point to the invisibility and erasure of the intellectual productivity of Black women in courses and colleges, as columnists in newspapers and on websites, as political authorities. These shared experiences reflect the ongoing relevance of the theory of a shared social location while acknowledging individual experience.

In virtual exchanges here in Brazil, we are used to hearing Hekman's same misunderstandings—"So-and-so is speaking from her own experience"—as though those experiences, despite containing lived knowledge from So-and-so's social location, are insufficient to make a genuine contribution to the question under discussion. As Collins argues, So-and-so's experience matters immensely, without a doubt: it can reveal crucial information about the social conditions that make up the group So-and-so belongs to, and which experiences this person shares within that group. To reduce feminist standpoint and speaking place theories to individual experience would be a huge mistake, for we have here a study of how structural oppressions prevent individual members *of certain groups* from having the right to speech, to humanity, *by virtue of their being part of those groups.*

The fact that people are Black does not mean that they will know how to reflect critically and philosophically on the consequences of racism. They may even say that they have never felt the effects of racism, that their experiences don't line up that way, or that they just never encountered it. But despite such people denying that they have experienced racism, they might still, because of their social location, have had access to fewer opportunities and rights. The discussion is, above all, structural, not "postmodern," as the theory's nay-sayers like to claim. The point is that these people misunderstand the issue and end up acting in an archetypically postmodern way, as Collins states, by reducing the concept to individual experiences instead of taking the social locus of the group into account.

For this reason, it is also misleading to suggest that the theory is invalidated by the fact that some individuals who oppose it are part of oppressed groups. It is precisely for this reason that Collins refuses to dismiss the individual point of view and instead emphasizes the social place an individual occupies within the matrix of domination. Any individual Black person might oppose standpoint theory and the idea of speaking place, but this does not mean that that Black person does not suffer racist oppression. The same holds true for other subaltern groups, and the opposite as well: no matter how conscientious people in privileged groups are, and how rigorously they combat oppressions, they still benefit, structurally speaking, from the oppressions their class inflicts on other groups. What we are questioning is the legitimacy conferred upon those belonging to the group located in power.

Obviously, individuals belonging to oppressed groups sometimes echo the discourses of the oppressor. We often see such individuals weaponized by those in power to delegitimize the larger fight against racism, sexism, and homophobia, or the theories themselves, whether feminist standpoint or speaking place. Instead of wasting energy talking about distinct individual experiences, as though statistics do not reflect human experience, a more responsible and ethical place to begin would be to discuss the fact that every twenty-three minutes, a Black youth is murdered in Brazil.[9] This example clearly illustrates how Black people as a socially and politically located group share the experience of state violence. Often, historically discriminated groups bear the full weight of advocating for change, for individuals in such groups face a greater demand to do so, as though they were more obligated than groups located within power to create strategies for confronting inequalities.

Social place does not automatically grant a discursive awareness of that place. The place we occupy socially does, however, give us distinct experiences and perspectives. Feminist standpoint theory and the concept of speaking place refute a universal vision of womanhood and of Blackness, and of other identities, just as it makes white men, who think of themselves as universal, recognize their own racial identities and reckon, as Grada Kilomba suggests, with what it means to be white as a metaphor for power. It also refutes the pretense of universality. By promoting a multiplicity of individual voices, listening to common experiences, and paying attention to what these individual and shared stories can tell us about the realities of the society we all inhabit, we seek to break with a single authorized discourse that claims to be universal. Above all, we endeavor to shatter the regime of discursive authorization.

Luiza Bairros, in "Our Feminisms Revisited," explains the importance of feminist standpoint theory:

According to [feminist standpoint] theory, the experience of sexist oppression is determined by the position we occupy in a matrix of domination where race, gender, and social class intersect at different points. To this way of thinking, a Black female worker is not triply oppressed or more oppressed than a white woman in the same social class, but rather experiences oppression from a place that provides a different standpoint on what it is like to be a woman in a racist and sexist society. Race, gender, social class, and sexual orientation mutually reconfigure one another to form what [Judith] Grant called a mosaic that can only be understood multidimensionally. According to feminist standpoint theory, then, there is no such thing as a single identity because the experience of being a woman is socially and historically determined. I consider this formulation particularly important not solely for the way it helps us understand different feminisms, but for how it allows us to think in terms of Black movements and Black women's movements in Brazil. This comes of the need to give expression to varied experiences of being Black (as lived through gender) and of being a woman (as lived through race) in a way that makes discussion of what should be the priority for the Black women's movement— fight sexism or fight racism?—superfluous, since these dimensions cannot be separated. From the point of view of both reflection and political action, one does not exist without the other.[10]

Bairros's explication is valuable because it helps us side-step what is commonly known as the "oppression Olympics." She teaches us that the debate is about the position each group occupies, given how race, gender, class, and sexuality crisscross to generate different experiences of oppression. We need to conceive of political actions and theories that can consider these intersections in tandem, rather than creating new hierarchies, since these dimensions cannot be considered independently.

I like to joke that I cannot say I'll fight racism and then tomorrow, at 2:25 p.m., if I have time, I'll fight sexism, since these oppressions act in concert. Being Black and a woman, I am put in a place of greater vulnerability because of these oppressions, and they must accordingly be combated together. Using Spivak, Alcoff, and Kilomba, let's delve deeper into this concept.[11]

Gayatri Spivak is central to our thinking about speaking place. Her essay *Can the Subaltern Speak?*, originally published in the 1980s with the subtitle "Speculations on Widow-Sacrifice," yields significant insights into how silence is imposed on the formerly colonized. Spivak is an important name in postcolonial thought, which, in brief, challenges and interrogates the foundations of dominant epistemologies and highlights knowledge produced by groups formerly subalternized in colonial territories. Spivak, as do Beauvoir and Kilomba, thinks about the Other as a category. In this essay, she takes up the difficulty contemporary French intellectuals have had in conceiving of the Other as a subject, since, according to her, they think of any "subject" as necessarily European.[12]

Even as a great interlocutor of Foucault, Spivak problematizes the fact that such writers as Foucault and the philosopher Gilles Deleuze do not depart entirely from the hegemonic discourse that takes Europe as the center of any

analysis: "It is impossible for contemporary French intellectuals to imagine the kind of Power and Desire that would
inhabit the unnamed subject of the Other of Europe. . . .
[E]verything they read, critical or uncritical, is caught within
the debate of the production of that Other, supporting or critiquing the constitution of the Subject as Europe."[13]

Spivak agrees with Foucault's thinking on the existence
of a system of power that disables, impedes, and invalidates
knowledge produced by subalternized groups. Foucault asserted that the masses could speak for themselves, but he
understood that there was a prohibition on those voices being heard. He believed that the role of the intellectual was to
analyze power relations, not to represent the people doing
battle. Spivak as a thinker believes that oppressed groups
can and should speak for themselves but asserts that Foucault thought of these groups only in the European context.
She cites, to illuminate her argument, the case of Indian
widows who were forced to self-immolate, a ritual called
sati, and who were in a place where it was much more difficult to speak for themselves. Moreover, for Spivak, intellectuals, in not being these oppressed subjects, "become
transparent in the relay race, for they merely report on the
non-represented subject and analyze (without analyzing)
the workings of (the unnamed Subject irreducibly presup-
posed by) power and desire."[14]

But then, who can speak?

> The subaltern cannot speak. There is no virtue in global
> laundry lists with "woman" as a pious term. Represen-
> tation has not withered away. The female intellectual as
> intellectual has a circumscribed task which she must not
> disown with a flourish.

Spivak boldly declares that because they are in a place where their humanity is not recognized, because they are classified as those who do not matter, subaltern groups do not have the right to a voice. But at the same time, she emphasizes the necessity of women's intellectual and political task. For her, the subaltern postulate reveals a silenced place.[15]

Does the subaltern never break the silence, though? Both Patricia Hill Collins and Grada Kilomba find Spivak's assertion on the subaltern's silence problematic if it is taken as absolute, and Spivak herself later retracted the declaration. For Collins and Kilomba, to think of this place as impossible to escape would be to legitimize the colonizer's norm, since it would attribute absolute power to the white-male-dominant discourse. Collins believes that validating this discourse as absolute would also mean believing that oppressed groups can identify only with the dominant discourse, that they will never be capable of their own reflections on the oppressive conditions imposed on them. It would also mean that any valid independent interpretation refuting the colonial discourse would be impossible to conceive.

In the previous chapter, we considered Collins's thinking on the necessity of Black women defining themselves. Such self-definition is an important strategy in confronting the colonial vision. And as we discussed in the first chapter, Black women have historically produced knowledge and dissent. Wouldn't putting them in a place where they never break the silence, with all the structurally imposed limits, be to confine them within the same logic they are fighting? The knowledge produced by members of historically discriminated groups, besides offering important counter-discourses, also offers new horizons of power, where the world is configured through other gazes and geographies.

The first chapter of Grada Kilomba's *Plantation Memories* contains an illustration, a picture of the slave Anastácia, who was forced to live with a mask covering her mouth. Kilomba explains that ostensibly, the mask was used to prevent enslaved Black persons from feeding themselves while they were forced to work on plantations, but it also served the function of imposing silence and fear, "inasmuch as the mouth was a place both of muteness and torture."[16] The Black Brazilian writer Conceição Evaristo, says, with respect to this image of the slave Anastácia, "I have frequently said that we know how to speak through openings in the mask and that sometimes we speak with such power that the mask is shattered. And I think that the shattering is one of our symbols, because our speaking forces off the mask."[17]

Apart from the specific question of this woman, who was forced to remain silent, to wear a device strapped across her mouth, Kilomba conceives of the mask as a distinctive marker of colonialism—a *"mask of speechlessness."* Seen this way, Kilomba asserts, this mask legitimizes the policy—or politics—of silencing Others. The questions she asks in this chapter are critical for our reflections on speech, place, and justice. "Who can speak?" she asks. "What happens when we speak?" and "What can we speak about?"[18]

This challenge is fundamental for our understanding of the speaking place. Within the project of colonization, who is authorized to speak? Does the fear imposed by those who created the masks impose limits on the silenced? To speak, oftentimes, leads to punishment and reprisal, and for just this reason, could it sometimes be preferable to agree with the hegemonic discourse as a way to survive? And if we speak, can we speak about anything and everything, or only on permitted topics? In a white supremacist patriarchal society, can white women, Black women, Black men, transgender persons, lesbians, and gays speak in the same way as cishet white men? Do they have the same space and legitimacy? Where space is made for a Black transgender woman to speak, for example, is she allowed to speak about economics or astrophysics, or only about being a Black transgender woman? Are knowledges constructed outside the academy considered knowledge? Kilomba provokes us to think about the nature of limits imposed within this colonial logic and makes us reflect on the consequences of the imposition of the mask of silence.

> The mask, therefore, raises many questions: Why must the mouth of the Black subject be fastened? Why must she or he be silenced? What could the Black subject say if her or his mouth were not sealed? And what would the *white* subject have to listen to? There is an apprehensive fear that if the colonial subject speaks, the colonizer will have to listen. She/he would be forced into an uncomfortable confrontation with "Other" truths. Truths that have been denied, repressed and kept quiet, as secrets. . . . Secrets like slavery. Secrets like colonialism. Secrets like racism.[19]

Kilomba touches on a theme essential to our discussion of speaking places: those who have always been authorized to speak need to listen. She posits that it is difficult for white people to do so because of the discomfort silenced voices bring, the confrontation that results from rupturing a unified vision of their place in the world. The stories of those forced into the place of the Other will necessarily surface conflicts we need to confront if change is to happen. To choose not to hear is to remain in a comfortable, snug place that awards the power to speak about *Others* even while those Others remain silenced.

Further, according to Kilomba, white people's "fear of listening to what could possibly be revealed by the Black subject can be articulated by Sigmund Freud's notion of repression," in the sense of avoiding something and holding it at a distance from consciousness. "Unpleasant ideas—and unpleasant truths—are rendered unconscious, out of awareness, due to the extreme anxiety, guilt or shame they cause." Further still: the white fear that manages to stay "unconscious" in the face of these realities, these truths, protects the white person from having to engage with knowledge of Others. Kilomba goes on to assert that, "once confronted by collective secrets and unpleasant truths of that very *dirty history,* the *white* subject commonly argues 'not to know . . . ,' 'not to understand . . . ,' 'not to remember . . . ,' 'not to believe . . . ,' or 'not to be convinced by.'"[20]

These expressions are part of the process of repression that keeps these truths from being remembered.

Talk of racism or gender oppression is generally seen as annoying, delegitimized as "chatter." And conscious recognition of what it means to destabilize the mainstream norm is seen as inappropriate or aggressive because it issues a direct challenge to power.

4
Everyone Has a Speaking Place

> My response to racism is anger. I have lived with that
> anger, ignoring it, feeding upon it, learning to use it
> before it laid my visions to waste, for most of my life.
> Once I did it in silence, afraid of the weight. My fear of
> anger taught me nothing. Your fear of that anger will
> teach you nothing, also.

—Audre Lorde

To name the places from which we speak disrupts the logic in which only the subaltern speaks from a social location, while those enmeshed in the fabric of the mainstream "norm" supposedly speak in universal terms. As the journalist and communications professor Rosane Borges notes, thinking about one's speaking place is an ethical posture, since "knowing the place we speak from is fundamental to thinking about hierarchies, inequality, poverty, racism, and sexism."[1]

Another criticism I often hear—and think is wrong-headed—is that the concept of speaking place aims to restrict the exchange of ideas, to close down discussion or impose a viewpoint. The artist and writer Jota Mombaça elucidates why this is incorrect:

There is a lot of talk about how this concept has been appropriated as a mode of granting or not granting authority to speak based on the positions and political identifiers that a specific body occupies in a world organized through the unequal distribution of violence and access. Critics who go this route apparently do not get that there is a politics (and police) of discursive authorization that predates the rupture advocated by speaking place activism. I mean, it's not as though speaking place activism is instituting the regime of authorization—quite the opposite. The regimes of discursive authorization are instituted against this activism, so that the political gesture of inviting a cis Euro-white man to be quiet and think before speaking introduces, in reality, a rupture in the regime of authorization already in force. If the concept of speaking place is forged into a tool for interrupting hegemonic voices, that is because it is being wielded to clear space for the possible emergence of historically interrupted voices. In this way, when speaking place activists deauthorize, they are ultimately deauthorizing the matrix of authority that constructed the world as an epistemic event, and also deauthorizing the fiction according to which we all have the same starting line, sharing equal access to speaking and listening.[2]

The multivocal attempt to disrupt the regime of authority provokes resistance in order to maintain this regime, to silence those voices. There is an attempt to say, "Get back in your place," since the group in power believes it has no corresponding place; its place is everywhere.

But the truth is that each person speaks from a specific

social, political, and historically inherited site of being and understanding. With this in mind, we can discuss and reflect critically on a wide variety of themes present in society. What is fundamental is that individuals belonging to social groups privileged by social locus are able to see the hierarchies produced from this place, as well as how this place directly impacts the makeup of the places of subalternized groups.

In a society like Brazil's, with its slavocratic heritage, Black individuals will experience racism from the hierarchical place of those who are objects of oppression—from the place of restricted opportunities that results from this system of oppression. White people will experience all this from the place of those who benefit from that same oppression. Thus, much as the two groups can and should discuss these questions, they are nonetheless speaking from distinct places. We simply demand that Brazil's history of slavery be told from our perspectives, and not only from those of the victors. We are pointing out the importance of breaking with the system in force, which obscures these narratives.

Despite its limits, the virtual world has become a viable medium for contesting narratives, where members of groups that have historically experienced discrimination find a place to exist, whether in the creation of pages or websites, or in blogs or video feeds.

The internet offers a kind of ultra-democratic space in which dominant narratives can be disputed and upended, but it is still less than ideal, owing to institutional barriers that impede access for dissenting voices. Just as self-expression is not a guaranteed right to all—it is still necessary to democratize other forms of mass media and break monopolies—discussion about freedom of expression cannot be grounded entirely on the right to express opinions, for that right is not absolute. But I want to stress that even within imposed limits, dissenting voices have managed to speak into concentrated communities of power, to make cracks in the narrative of those in power, a narrative that often, dishonestly, accuses those voices of aggressiveness when in reality they are merely fighting the violence of this imposed silence. The group that has always held power, in an inversion of logic and a false symmetry caused by the fear of sharing spaces that they have previously controlled, is made uncomfortable by the raising of those voices. Even despite these cracks, we must nevertheless continue this structural debate, since the one does not definitively rule out the other.

In a stage performance produced in Brazil in 2016 called *Decolonizing Knowledge,* Grada Kilomba simply and brilliantly describes the importance of disrupting hierarchies instituted by the authorized discourse:

> The structures of knowledge validation, which define what "true" and "valid" scholarship is, are controlled by *white* scholars, both male and female, who declare their perspectives' universal requirement. . . . Any scholarship that does not convey the Eurocentric order of knowledge has been continuously rejected on the grounds that it does not constitute credible science. Science is, in this sense, not a simple apolitical study of truth, but the reproduction of racial power relations that define what counts as true and in whom to believe. . . .
>
> As a scholar, for instance, I am commonly told that my

work on everyday racism is very interesting, but not really scientific, a remark that illustrates the colonial order in which Black scholars reside: "You have a very *subjective* perspective"; "very *personal*"; "very *emotional*"; "very *specific*"; "Are these *objective facts?*"

Interesting, but *unscientific;* interesting, but *subjective;* interesting, but *personal, emotional* and *partial:* "You do *over-interpret,*" said a colleague. "You must think you are *the queen of interpretation.*"

Such comments function like a mask that silences our voices as soon as we speak. They allow the *white* subject to place our discourses back at the margins, as deviating knowledge, while their discourses remain at the centre, as the norm. When they speak it is scientific, when we speak it is unscientific:

universal/specific;
objective/subjective;
neutral/personal;
rational/emotional;
impartial/partial;
they have facts, we have opinions
they have knowledge, we have experiences.

These are not simple semantic categorizations; they possess a dimension of power that maintains hierarchical positions and upholds *white* supremacy. We are not dealing here with a "peaceful coexistence of words," as Jacques Derrida emphasizes, but rather a violent hierarchy that defines *who can speak.*[3]

We can see from Kilomba's passage that there are similarities of thought among the main writers cited here. All of them refute epistemological neutrality in favor of the need to recognize diverse knowledges and the importance of understanding these as localized, as well as the importance of disrupting an axiom of silence. As we have seen, Lélia Gonzalez, Linda Alcoff, Gayatri Spivak, and others emphasize the need to break with the dominant epistemology and center the debate on identity, taking into account how institutional power defines identities so as to oppress them and bring them in line. To think about speaking places, for these thinkers, is to destabilize, to create fissures and tensions that might lead to the emergence of new ways of seeing, not solely of counter-discourses, given that "counter" means being against something: to be "counter-hegemonic" is still to orient by that which is imposed on me.

Yes, the discourses brought by these writers are counter-hegemonic in the sense of aiming to destabilize the norm, but they are also powerful discourses in their own rights, built around entirely different reference points and geographies. These writers are coming up with other ways of being, outside those imposed by the dominant discursive regime. They are not imposing some "true" epistemology but rather calling for reflection. The works of the various authors presented here reveal oppressions suffered by different groups as their rights continue to be restricted. What puts certain groups in subaltern positions is not a categorical imperative, a should-be, but rather an unveiling of historical processes.

To consider a speaking place is to disrupt the institutional silencing of the subalternized; it is to move toward breaking with hierarchy, which Derrida appropriately diagnosed as violent.[4]

There are people who say that the cause is what matters, or some imaginary voice of justice from the ether, as though we are not embodied, marked, and delegitimized by the norms of colonization. But it is only those who always had a voice, who never needed to reclaim their humanity and whose humanity was always taken for granted who have the luxury of pretending that voices are not embodied. Our voices are rooted in the places where we stand.

As we began, so we end, with Lélia Gonzalez: "The trash will speak, and we don't care what you think."

Notes

Quotations from sources originally published in Portuguese or French are translated by Padma Viswanathan. Online Portuguese sources can usually be accessed in English translation.

INTRODUCTION

1. "Protagonism" is a term of use in Latin American feminism; the Canadian scholar Janet M. Conway, who uses the term in English, defined it in an email to the translator as "sustained and self-conscious action, initiative, or leadership undertaken by collective political subjects."

2. See Regina Dalcastagnè, *Literatura Brasileira contemporânea: Um território contestado* (São Paulo: Editora Horizonte, 2012).

1. A BRIEF HISTORY LESSON

Epigraph: Lélia Gonzalez, "Racismo e sexismo na cultura brasileira," 225.

1. While some have felt Marcus Robinson's version might be more accurate to Sojourner Truth's way of speaking, Frances Gage did publish her version during the activist's lifetime, and it is this version that has reverberated in Black feminist thinking, so I have chosen to quote that version here, though with the spelling normalized from Gage's version, which attempted to represent her dialect. For a comparison of the two speeches, see Truth, "Her Words."

2. "Women's Rights Convention: Sojourner Truth."

3. According to the dominant view of feminism, history is divided into three waves with very specific qualities—from 1792, when Mary

Wollstonecraft published *A Vindication of the Rights of Woman* to 1960; 1960–1980; 1990–present—though this vision is contested by Black and white feminists, such as Clare Hemmings, who, in "Telling Feminist Stories," says that "despite feminist theory's clear variety, both within and outside 'the West,' when telling its own recent story a dominant narrative, albeit one with a range of affective or critical inflections, does emerge. That story divides the recent past into clear decades to provide a narrative of relentless progress or loss, proliferation or homogenization" (115). I also recommend, as further reading, *Breve história do feminismo no Brasil,* by Maria Amélia de Almeida Teles.

4. "Intersectionality" is a term coined by legal scholar and activist Kimberlé Crenshaw denoting the ways the multiple social identities or categories occupied by a given individual interact to determine experiences of discrimination or privilege. The Black intellectual bell hooks, born Gloria J. Watkins, took her grandmother's name and prefers that it be written in lowercase.

5. Xavier, "Feminismo."

6. Truth, "Convention Wisdom."

7. Harriet Jacobs, like Sojourner Truth, was a formerly enslaved woman who fought in the American abolitionist movement. She published an autobiography titled *Incidents in the Life of a Slave Girl* under the pseudonym Linda Brent, in which she told of the abuses and violence suffered by enslaved Black people.

8. Gonzalez, "A categoria político-cultural de amefricanidade," 71. Donna Haraway maintains that all knowledge is "situated" (socially and historically) and, therefore, partial. This is not to say that for Haraway it is necessary to abandon any and all "objective" criteria. To the contrary, Haraway seeks to strengthen a notion of objectivity as opposed to agreement with a postmodern feminist critique. See Haraway, "Situated Knowledges."

9. The feminist Gloria Anzaldúa also proposes a rebellion against normative grammar in favor of a Chicano alternative. "Chicano Spanish is a border tongue which developed naturally. Change, *evolución, enriquecimiento de palabras nuevas por invención o adopción* have created

variants of Chicano Spanish, *um nuevo lenguaje. Un lenguaje que corres-
ponde a un modo de vivir.* Chicano Spanish is not incorrect, it's a living
language." Anzaldúa, "How to Tame a Wild Tongue," 55.

10. For more on this see hooks, *Teaching to Transgress.*

11. Gonzalez, "Racismo e sexismo na cultura brasileira," 238.

12. Alcoff, "An Epistemology for the Next Revolution," 68.

13. hooks, "Black Women Intellectuals."

14. Alcoff, "An Epistemology for the Next Revolution," 72–73.

2. THE BLACK WOMAN

Epigraph: *Narrative of Sojourner Truth, a Northern Slave,* 112.

1. Beauvoir means bad faith in a strict Sartrean sense. For Jean-
Paul Sartre, bad faith is the attempt to exempt oneself from responsibility to the point of reducing oneself to pure thingness (in-itself). It is
to become passive and attribute one's actions to temperament; to adopt
a religion and accept its dogmas; or even to claim to have a certain per-
sonality on account of race or gender. It is not a lie in which a person
hides the truth from someone else, but when one hides it from oneself.
"Bad faith . . . as we have said, is lying *to oneself.* That is to say, for he who
practices bad faith, it is a question of masking a disagreeable truth or
presenting an agreeable inaccuracy as truth. Bad faith has, in this way,
the structure of a lie. Except—and this changes everything—with bad
faith, I hide the truth from myself." Sartre, *L'être et le néant,* 83.

2. Beauvoir, *La deuxième sexe,* 16, citing Claude Lévi-Strauss, *Les
structure élémentaires de la parenté* (Paris: Presses Universitaires de
France, 1949; available in English as *The Elementary Structures of Kin-
ship,* trans. James Harle Bell, John Richard von Sturmer, and Rodney
Needham, editor [Boston: Beacon, 1969]).

3. Kilomba, *Plantation Memories,* 54, quoting Mirza, *Black British
Feminism,* 4, with "maintained" substituted for "sustained," and "Blacks"
capitalized.

4. Kilomba, *Plantation Memories.*

5. The category of Black men is also diverse and intersected by demarcations including sexuality, gender identity, and class, among others. In our book series Plural Feminisms/Feminismos Plurais, we address themes of Black masculinities.

6. On the pay differential between Black women and white men in São Paulo, see "Research Points Out Inequality in the Average Salary of Black Women in SP"; on the differential in the United States, see Kochhar, "The Enduring Grip of the Gender Pay Gap."

7. See Waiselfisz, *Mapa da violência 2015.*

8. Werneck, "Nossos passos vêm de longe!"

9. Beauvoir, *La deuxième sexe,* 28.

10. See Lima, "Mulheres militantes negras."

11. Collins, "Learning from the Outsider Within," S18.

12. Ibid., S14. Luiza Bairros in "Nossos feminismos revisitados" [Our Feminisms Revisited] also offers an interesting perspective based on Black women in domestic employment.

13. Collins, "Learning from the Outsider Within," S14.

14. Carneiro, "Enegrecer o feminismo," 50–51, quoting Linda Alcoff and Elizabeth Potter, " Introduction: When Feminisms Intersect Epistemology," in Alcoff and Potter, *Feminist Epistemologies,* 3–4.

15. Sebastião, "Feminismo negro e suas práticas no campo da cultura." Lélia Gonzalez is among those debating these issues: "The fact is that, as Black women, we felt the need to deepen our reflections, instead of continually repeating and reproducing models offered to us by social science research. The texts only talked about Black women from a socioeconomic perspective that elucidated a series of problems posed by race relations. But there was still (and will still be) a portion remaining that defied explanation." See Gonzalez, "Racismo e sexismo na cultura brasileira."

16. Lorde, "The Master's Tools Will Never Dismantle the Master's House," 112; Lorde, "Age, Race, Class, and Sex," 123.

17. Lorde, "The Master's Tools Will Never Dismantle the Master's House," 112.

3. WHAT IS A SPEAKING PLACE?

Epigraph: Suheir Hammad, *Born Palestinian, Born Black* (Brooklyn, N.Y.: UpSet Press, 2010). Reprinted by permission of UpSet Press.

1. "It appears to me that in any society, the production of discourse is simultaneously controlled, selected, organized and redistributed by a certain number of procedures whose function is to ward off its powers and dangers, to gain mastery over its randomness, to dodge its heavy, dreadful materiality." Foucault, *L'ordre du discours,* 2.

2. Amaral, "Lugares de fala," 105; "The concept of speaking places was constructed in [Amaral's] doctoral thesis, "Lugares de fala do leitor no Diário Gaúcho" [Speaking places of the Diário Gaúcho reader], to analyze a popular, mainstream newspaper whose popularization strategies are not reducible to sensationalism" (ibid., 104).

3. Ibid., 104.

4. Collins, "Comment on Hekman's 'Truth and Method: Feminist Standpoint Theory Revisited,'" 375.

5. Ibid., 376.

6. Ibid., 377.

7. Brazilian Report, "Slavery in Brazil," May 13, 2020, "Brazil Builds" blog post of the Brazil Institute, Wilson Center, https://www.wilsoncenter.org/blog-post/slavery-brazil#:~:text=On%20May%2013%2C%201888%2C%20Brazilian,slavery%20in%20all%20its%20forms (accessed July 11, 2023); Teixeira, *Trabalho Doméstico.*

8. Nugent, "'We Can't Take It Anymore.'"

9. Marília Marques, "'A cada 23 minutos, um jovem negro morre no Brasil,' diz ONU ao lançar campanha contra violência," July 11, 2017, Distrito Federal, https://g1.globo.com/distrito-federal/noticia/a-cada-23-minutos-um-jovem-negro-morre-no-brasil-diz-onu-ao-lancar-campanha-contra-violencia.ghtml.

10. Bairros, "Nossos feminismos revisitados," 461, citing Judith Grant, *Fundamental Feminism: Contesting the Core Concepts of Feminist Theory* (New York: Routledge, 1991).

11. As I said previously, beyond the conceptualization given by people in the communications field, there is no certainty around the concept's origin point, properly speaking, nor any established epistemology. Our hypothesis is that, based on the work of the authors cited here, it is possible to conceptualize and expand our understanding.

12. "The Other as Subject is inaccessible to Foucault and Deleuze": Spivak, "Can the Subaltern Speak?" (rev. ed.), 37.

13. Ibid., 35. "What intellectuals have realized since the recent upheaval is that the masses do not need them for knowledge; they apprehend perfectly, clearly, much better than the intellectuals, and say so quite well. But there is a system of power that blocks, forbids, and invalidates this speech and this knowledge. . . . The role of the intellectual is no longer to put himself 'a little ahead or a little to the side' so as to speak the silenced truth of everything; it is instead to fight those forms of power making him their object and instrument in the order of 'knowledge,' 'truth,' 'consciousness,' and 'discourse.' " Foucault and Deleuze, "Les intellectuels et le pouvoir."

14. Spivak, "Appendix: Can the Subaltern Speak?" 248.

15. Ibid., 283.

16. Kilomba, *Plantation Memories,* 14. Anastácia's African name is unknown. No reliable historical information on her origins is available, but it is believed that Anastácia was the daughter of King Kimbundo, born in present-day Angola, and brought by force to Bahia, in northeastern Brazil, during slavery, or that she was a Nagô/Yorubá princess before being enslaved.

17. [Ribeiro], "Conceição Evaristo."

18. Kilomba, *Plantation Memories,* 14.

19. Ibid., 19.

20. Ibid., 19, 20. *Dirty history* is an expression used by the writer Toni Morrison, the first Black woman to win the Nobel Prize in Literature, in 1993. Morrison described her work as bringing into light the "dirty business of racism" (ibid., 21).

4. EVERYONE HAS A SPEAKING PLACE

Epigraph: Audre Lorde, "The Uses of Anger."

1. Rosane Borges, quoted in Moreira and Dias, "O que é 'lugar de fala' e como ele é aplicado no debate público?"

2. Mombaça, "Notas estratégicas quanto ao uso politico do conceito de lugar de fala." Sueli Carneiro adds, "This process of social banishment is coupled with exclusion from educational opportunities, the primary means of social mobility in our country. In this dynamic, for those who have been racially oppressed, the educational system is almost entirely built to be a source of multiple processes of annihilation—of cognitive capacities and intellectual confidence. This phenomenon transpires through the lowering of self-esteem perpetrated daily in school by racism and discrimination; through the erasure of Blacks as subjects of knowledge; through devaluing, denying, or concealing the contributions of Africa and the African diaspora to human cultural heritage; through the imposition of cultural whitening; and through causing students to fail and drop out of school. We call these processes epistemicide." Carneiro, "Epistemicídio."

3. Adapted from Kilomba, *Decolonizing Knowledge,* quoting Derrida, *Positions,* 41, with "peaceful coexistence of words" substituted for "peaceful coexistence of a *vis-à-vis.*"

4. Derrida, *Positions.*

Bibliography

Alcoff, Linda, and Elizabeth Potter, eds. *Feminist Epistemologies.* New York: Routledge, 1993.

Alcoff, Linda Martín. "An Epistemology for the Next Revolution." *Transmodernity: Journal of Peripheral Cultural Production of the Luso-Hispanic World* 1, no. 2 (2011): 67–78. Available online: http://dx.doi .org/10.5070/T412011808. Portuguese language version: "Uma epistemologia para a próxima revolução." *Sociedade e Estado* 31, no. 1(2016): 129–143. Trans. Cristina Patriota de Moura. Available online: https:// www.researchgate.net/publication/302983379_Uma_epistemologia _para_a_proxima_revolucao.

Amaral, Márcia Franz. "Lugares de fala: Um conceito para abordar o segmento popular da grande imprensa [Speaking Places: A Concept to Address the Popular Segment of the Mainstream Press]." *Contracampo* 12 (January–July 2005): 103–114. Available online: https:// periodicos.uff.br/contracampo/article/view/17388.

Anzaldúa, Gloria. "How to Tame a Wild Tongue." In *Borderlands La Frontera: The New Mestiza,* 53–64. San Francisco: Aunt Lute Books, 1987. Available online: https://english.washington.edu/sites/english /files/documents/ewp/teaching_resources/anzaldua_how_to_tame _a_wild_tongue.pdf. Portuguese language version: "Como domar uma língua selvagem." *Cadernos de Letras da UFF* 39 (2009): 297–309. Available online: https://www.yumpu.com/pt/document/view /12544587/como-domar-uma-lingua-selvagem-gloria-anzaldua-uff.

Bairros, Luiza. "Mulher negra: O reforço da subordinação [Black Woman: Reinforcing Subordination]." In *Desigualdade racial no Brasil contemporâneo [Racial Inequality in Brazil Today],* ed. P. Lovell. Belo Horizonte: UFMG/ CEDEPLAR, 1991.

Bairros, Luiza. "Nossos feminismos revisitados [Our Feminisms Revisited]." In *Revista Estudos Feministas* 3, no. 2 (1995): 458–463.

Beauvoir, Simone de. *La deuxième sexe*. Paris: Gallimard, 1949. Portuguese language version: *O segundo sexo: Fatos e mitos [The Second Sex: Facts and Myths]*. Trans. Sérgio Milliet. 4th ed. São Paulo: Difusão Europeia do Livro, 1980. English language version: *The Second Sex*. Trans. Constance Borde and Sheila Malovany-Chevallier. New York: Vintage, 2011.

Benjamin, Walter. "Sobre conceito da história." In *Magia e técnica, arte e política: Ensaios sobre literatura e história da cultura [Magic and Craft, Art and Politics: Essays on Literature and Cultural History]*. Trans. Sérgio Paulo Rouanet. 3rd ed. São Paulo: Brasiliense, 1987. Obras escolhidas, vol. 1. Available online: https://psicanalisepolitica.files.word press.com/2014/10/obras-escolhidas-vol-1-magia-e-tc3a9cnica-arte -e-polc3adtica.pdf. English language version: "Theses on the Philosophy of History." In Benjamin, *Illuminations*. Trans. Harry Zohn. Boston: Mariner, 2019.

Brah, Avtar. "Difference, Diversity, Differentiation." In Brah, *Cartographies of Diaspora: Contesting Identities*, 95–126. London: Routledge, 1996. Portuguese language version: "Diferença, diversidade, diferenciação." *Cadernos Pagu* 26 (January–June 2006): 329–376.

Carneiro, Sueli. "Enegrecer o feminismo: A situação da mulher negra na América Latina a partir de uma perspectiva de gênero [Blackening Feminism: The Situation of Black Women in Latin America from a Gender Perspective]." In *Racismos contemporâneos*, ed. Ashoka Social Entrepreneurship and Takano Citizenship, 50–51. Rio de Janeiro: Takano Editora, 2003).

Carneiro, Sueli, "Epistemicídio [Epistemicide]." *Portal Geledés* (September 4, 2014). Available online: https://www.geledes.org.br/epistemi cidio/.

Collins, Patricia Hill. *Black Feminist Thought: Knowledge, Consciousness and the Politics of Empowerment*. New York: Routledge, 2000.

Collins, Patricia Hill. "Comment on Hekman's 'Truth and Method: Feminist Standpoint Theory Revisited': Where's the Power?" *Signs* 22, no. 2 (1997): 375–381. Available online: https://www.jstor.org/stable /3175278. Portuguese language version: "Comentário sobre o artigo de Hekman 'Truth and Method: Feminist Standpoint Theory Revisited': Onde está o poder?" *Signs* 22, no. 2 (1997): 375–381. Trans. Juliana Borges.

Crenshaw, Kimberlé. "Demarginalizing the Intersection of Race and Sex: A Black Feminist Critique of Antidiscrimination Doctrine, Feminist Theory, and Antiracist Politics." *University of Chicago Legal Forum* 1989, no. 1, article 8 (1989): 139–167. Available online: https:// chicagounbound.uchicago.edu/cgi/viewcontent.cgi?article=1052& context=uclf.

Crenshaw, Kimberlé. "Documento para o encontro de especialistas em aspectos da discriminação racial relativos ao gênero [Background Paper for the Expert Meeting on Gender-Related Aspects of Race Discrimination]." *Revista Estudos Feministas,* 10th year (January–July 2002). Available online: https://edisciplinas.usp.br/pluginfile.php /4123084/mod_resource/content/1/Crenshaw%202002%20revista %20estudos%20feministas.pdf.

Dalcastagnè, Regina. *Literatura Brasileira contemporânea: Um território contestado.* São Paulo: Editora Horizonte, 2012.

Derrida, Jacques. *Positions.* Trans. Alan Bass. Chicago: University of Chicago Press, 1981.

Foucault, Michel, and Gilles Deleuze. "Les intellectuels et le pouvoir." *Dits Ecrits.* Book 2, Text 106 (March 2, 1972): 3–10. Available online: http://1libertaire.free.fr/MFoucault110.html. English language version: "Intellectuals and Power: A Discussion Between Michel Foucault and Gilles Deleuze." Trans. Mark Seem. *Telos* 1973, no. 16 (1973): 103–9. Available online: doi: 10.3817/0673016103.

Foucault, Michel. *L'ordre du discours.* Paris: Gallimard, 1971. English language version: "The Discourse on Language." In *The Archaeology of Knowledge and the Discourse on Language.* Trans. A. M. Sheridan Smith. 215–38. New York: Pantheon, 1972.

Gonzalez, Lélia. "A categoria político-cultural de amefricanidade." *Tempo Brasileiro* 92/93 (January–June 1988): 69–82.

Gonzalez, Lélia. "Racismo e sexismo na cultura brasileira." *Revista Ci-
ências Sociais Hoje,* Anpocs (1984): 223–244. Available online: https://
ria.ufrn.br/jspui/handle/123456789/2298. English language version:
Lélia Gonzalez, Bruna Barros, Feva, Jess Oliveira, and Luciana Reis.
"Racism and Sexism in Brazilian Culture." *WSQ: Women's Studies
Quarterly* 49 (2021): 371–394. Available online: doi:10.1353/wsq.2021
.0027.

Gushiken, Luiz. *Comunicação pública.* Ed. Maria José da Costa Oliveira.
Campinas: Alínea Editora, 2014.

Hall, Stuart. "Cultural Identity and Diaspora." In *Identity: Community,
Culture, Difference,* ed. Jonathan Rutherford. London: Lawrence and
Wishart, 1990.

Hall, Stuart. *Da diáspora: Identidades e mediações culturais [Of the Diaspora: Identities and Cultural Mediations].* Ed. Liv Sovick. Trans. Ade-
laine La Guardia Resende . . . [et al]. Belo Horizonte: Editora UFMG,
2009.

Haraway, Donna, "Situated Knowledges: The Science Question in Feminism and the Privilege of Partial Perspective." *Feminist Studies*
14, no. 3 (1988): 575–599. Available online: https://doi.org/10.2307
/3178066. Portuguese language version: "Saberes localizados: A
questão da ciência para o feminismo e o privilégio da perspectiva
parcial." *Cadernos Pagu* 5 (1995): 7–41. Available online: https://www
.copene2018.eventos.dype.com.br/resources/anais/8/1524482904
_ARQUIVO_DonnaHarawaysaberessituados.pdf.

Hemmings, Clare. "Telling Feminist Stories." *Feminist Theory* 6 (2005):
115–244. Available online: https://doi.org/10.1177/1464700105053690.
Portuguese language version: "Contando estórias feministas." *Revista Estudos Feministas* 17, no. 1 (January–April 2009): 215–241.
Trans. Ramayana Lira. Ed. Claudia de Lima Costa. Available online:
https://www.jstor.org/stable/24327586.

hooks, bell. "Black Women Intellectuals." In bell hooks and Cornel
West, *Breaking Bread: Insurgent Black Intellectual Life,* 147–164. New
York: Routledge, 2016.

hooks, bell. *Feminism Is for Everybody: Passionate Politics.* London: Pluto Press, 2000.

hooks, bell. *Talking Back: Thinking Feminist and Thinking Black.* Boston: South End Press, 1989.

hooks, bell. *Teaching to Transgress: Education as the Practice of Freedom.* New York: Routledge, 1994.

Kilomba, Grada. *Decolonizing Knowledge: Lecture Performance, March 24, 2016, Cologne Academy,* Akademie der Künst der Welt, https://www.adkdw.org/en/article/937_decolonizing_knowledge.

Kilomba, Grada. *Plantation Memories: Episodes of Everyday Racism.* Münster: Unrast-Verlag, 2012.

Kochhar, Rakesh. "The Enduring Grip of the Gender Pay Gap." March 1, 2023. Pew Research Center, https://www.pewresearch.org/social-trends/2023/03/01/the-enduring-grip-of-the-gender-pay-gap/.

Lima, Ana Nery Correia. "Mulheres militantes negras: A interseccionalidade de gênero e raça na produção das identidades contemporâneas [Militant Black Women: Intersectionality of Gender and Race in the Production of Contemporary Identities]." In *Summary of the 2nd International Interdisciplinary Conference on the Social Sciences and Humanities (2013),* 15–27. Available online: https://poligen.polignu.org/sites/poligen.polignu.org/files/feminismo%20negro.pdf.

Lorde, Audre. "Age, Race, Class, and Sex: Women Redefining Difference." In Lorde, *Sister Outsider: Essays and Speeches,* 114–123. Berkeley: Crossing Press, 2007.

Lorde, Audre. "The Master's Tools Will Never Dismantle the Master's House." Comments at the "The Personal and the Political Panel," *Second Sex Conference,* New York, September 29, 1979. In Lorde, *Sister Outsider: Essays and Speeches,* 110–113. Berkeley: Crossing Press, 2007. Portuguese language version: "Mulheres negras: As ferramentas do mestre nunca irão desmantelar a casa do mestre." Trans. Renata. *Portal Geledés,* October 7, 2013. Available online: https://www

.geledes.org.br/mulheres-negras-as-ferramentas-do-mestre-nunca
-irao-desmantelar-a-casa-do-mestre/.

Lorde, Audre, "The Uses of Anger: Women Responding to Racism." Keynote presentation at the National Women's Studies Association Conference, Storrs, Connecticut, 1981. Portuguese language version: "Os usos da raiva: mulheres respondendo ao racismo." Trans. Renata. *Portal Geledés,* May 19, 2013. Available online: https://www.geledes .org.br/os-usos-da-raiva-mulheres-respondendo-ao-racismo/ (accessed September 28, 2017).

Mirza, Heidi Safia, ed. *Black British Feminism: A Reader.* London: Routledge, 1997.

Mombaça, Jota. "Notas estratégicas quanto ao uso politico do conceito de lugar de fala [Strategic Notes on the Political Use of the Concept of Speaking Place]." *Buala,* July 19, 2017. Available online: https:// www.buala.org/pt/corpo/notas-estrategicas-quanto-aos-usos -politicos-do-conceito-de-lugar-de-fala.

Moreira, Matheus, and Tatiana Dias. "O que é 'lugar de fala' e como ele é aplicado no debate público? [What Is 'Speaking Place' and How Is It Applied in Public Debate?]." *Nexo Journal* (January 16, 2017). Available online: https://www.nexojornal.com.br/expresso/2017/01/15/O -que-é-'lugar-de-fala'-e-como-ele-é-aplicado-no-debate-público.

Narrative of Sojourner Truth, a Northern Slave. Boston: Printed for the author, 1850.

Negrão, T. "Feminismo no plural [Feminism in the Plural]." In *As mulheres e a filosofia [Women and Philosophy],* ed. M. Tiburi, M. M. Menezes, and E. Eggert, 271–280. São Leopoldo: UNISINOS, 2002.

Nugent, Ciara. "'We Can't Take It Anymore.' How the Death of a 5-Year-Old Boy Has Spurred Brazil's Black Domestic Workers to Fight for Better Treatment." *Time* (July 17, 2020). Available online: https:// time.com/5867784/black-domestic-workers-treatment-brazil/.

Pinheiro, Luana Simões, Antonio Teixeira Lima, Jr., Natália de Oliveira Fontoura, and Rosane da Silva. "Mulheres e trabalho: Breve análise do período 2004–2014 [Women and Work: A Brief Analysis of 2004–

2014]." *Ipea* 24 (March 2016). Available online: https://repositorio
.ipea.gov.br/handle/11058/6524.

Piscitelli, Adriana. "Interseccionalidades, categorias de articulação e
experiências de migrantes brasileiras [Intersectionalities, Articulation Categories and Experiences of Brazilian Migrants]." *Sociedade e
Cultura* 11, no. 2 (July–December 2008): 263–274.

Prá, J. R. "O feminismo como teoria e como prática [Feminism as Theory and Practice]." In *Mulher: estudos de gênero,* ed. M. Strey, 39–57.
São Leopoldo: UNISINOS, 1997.

"Research Points Out Inequality in the Average Salary of Black Women
in SP." March 8, 2023. SEADE, https://www.seade.gov.br/pesquisa
-aponta-desigualdade-na-media-salarial-da-mulher-negra-em-sp/.

[Ribeiro, Djamila]. "Conceição Evaristo: 'Nossa fala estilhaça a máscara
do silêncio' [Conceição Evaristo: Our Speech Shatters the Mask of
Silence]." *Carta Capital* (May 13, 2017). Available online: https://www
.cartacapital.com.br/sociedade/conceicao-evaristo-201cnossa-fala
-estilhaca-a-mascara-do-silencio201d/.

Sartre, Jean-Paul. *L'être et le néant: Essai d'ontologie phénoménologique.*
Paris: Gallimard, 1943. Portuguese language version: *O ser e o nada:
Ensaio de ontologia fenomenológica.* Trans. Paulo Perdigão. Petrópo-
lis: Vozes, 1997. English language version: *Being and Nothingness: An
Essay on Phenominological Ontology.* Trans. Sarah Richmond. New
York: Washington Square Press, 1943.

Sebastião, Ana Angélica. "Feminismo negro e suas práticas no campo
da cultura [Black Feminism and Its Practices in the Culture Camp]."
ABPN Journal 1, no. 1 (March–June 2010).

Sotero, Edilza Correia. "Transformações no acesso ao ensino superior
brasileiro: Algumas implicações para os diferentes grupos de cor
e sexo [Transformations in Access to Brazilian Higher Education:
Some Implications for Different Gender and Race Groups]." In *Dos-
siê mulheres negras: Retrato das condições de vida das mulheres negras
no Brasil [Dossier on Black Women: A Portrait of Black Women's Living
Conditions in Brazil],* ed. Mariana Mazzini Marcondes et al., 37–52.
Brasília: Ipea, 2013.

Spivak, Gayatri. "Can the Subaltern Speak?" (rev. ed.) and "Appendix: Can the Subaltern Speak?" In *Can the Subaltern Speak?: Reflections on the History of an Idea*, ed. Rosalind C. Morris, 21–78, 237–291. New York: Columbia University Press, 2010. Portuguese language version: *Pode o subalterno falar?* Belo Horizonte: Editora UFMG, 2010.

Teixeira, Juliana. *Trabalho Doméstico [Domestic Work]*. São Paulo: Jandaira/Feminismos Plurais, 2021.

Teles, Maria Amélia de Almeida. *Breve história do feminismo no Brasil [A Brief History of Feminism in Brazil]*. São Paulo: Alameda, 2017.

Toledo, Cecília. *Mulheres: O gênero nos une, a classe nos divide [Women: Gender Unites Us, Class Divides Us]*. 2nd ed. São Paulo: José Luís e Rosa Sundermann, 2003.

Truth, Sojourner. "Ain't I a Woman? December 1851." Internet Modern History Sourcebook, Fordham University, http://www.fordham.edu /halsall/mod/sojtruth-woman.asp.

Truth, Sojourner. "Convention Wisdom." *Lapham's Quarterly*. Available online: https://www.laphamsquarterly.org/fashion/convention -wisdom.

Truth, Sojourner. "Her Words: Sojourner's Words and Music." Sojourner Truth Memorial Committee, https://sojournertruthmemorial.org /sojourner-truth/her-words/ (accessed August 31, 2022).

Waiselfisz, Julio Jacobo. *Mapa da violência 2015: Homicídio de mulheres no Brasil [Violence Map, 2015: Murders of Brazilian Women]*. FLASCO Brasil, November 9, 2015. Available online: https://www .onumulheres.org.br/wp-content/uploads/2016/04/MapaViolencia _2015_mulheres.pdf.

Werneck, Jurema. "Nossos passos vêm de longe! Movimentos de mulheres negras e estratégias políticas contra o sexismo e o racismo [We Come from Afar! Black Women's Movements and Political Strategies for Fighting Sexism and Racism]." In *Vents d'Est, vents d'Ouest: Mouvements de femmes et féminismes anticoloniaux [Winds from the East, Winds from the West: Anticolonial Women's and Feminist Movements]*. Geneva: Graduate Institute Publications, 2009. Available on-

line: http://books.openedition.org/iheid/6316 and https://doi.org/10
.4000/books.iheid.6316.

"Women's Rights Convention: Sojourner Truth." In *Anti-Slavery Bugle*,
June 21, 1851, Library of Congress, Chronicling America, https://
chroniclingamerica.loc.gov/lccn/sn83035487/1851-06-21/ed-1/seq-4/.

Xavier, Giovana. "Feminismo: Direitos autorais de uma prática linda e
preta [Feminism: Copyright of a Beautiful Black Practice]." *Folha de
S.Paulo* (July 19, 2017). Available online: https://agoraequesaoelas
.blogfolha.uol.com.br/2017/07/19/feminismo-uma-pratica-linda-e
-preta/.

Translator's Acknowledgments

The translator offers many thanks to Vincent Blevins, My'Kayla Bowser, Edvan Brito, Geoffrey Brock, Desirée Santos, Vega Subramaniam, and the members of the Portuguese-English Literary Translators' Association for consultation and advice.

DJAMILA RIBEIRO is a political philosopher, essayist, journalist, and one of the most influential leaders in the Afro-Brazilian women's rights movement. She is the director of the Plural Feminisms Project, which includes the Plural Feminisms book series and the Plural Feminisms Space, which supports women experiencing social vulnerability in São Paulo. She is the author of five books: *Where We Stand, Who's Afraid of Black Feminism?, Letters to My Grandmother, A Short Antiracist Manual,* and *Transatlantic Dialogue.* She is a laureate of the 2019 Prince Claus Prize, awarded by the Netherlands, and was named one of the one hundred most influential women in the world by the BBC that same year. In 2020, she won the Jabuti Award, the most important honor in Brazilian literature, and in 2021, she was the first Brazilian to receive the Black Entertainment Television International Global Good Award. In 2023 she received the Franco-German Prize for Human Rights and the Rule of Law.

PADMA VISWANATHAN is a novelist, playwright, and translator whose translations from the Portuguese include *São Bernardo* by Graciliano Ramos (2020). She is the author of four books—*The Charterhouse of Padma* (2024), *Like Every Form of Love: A Memoir of Friendship and True Crime* (2023), *The Ever After of Ashwin Rao* (2014), and *The Toss of a Lemon* (2008)—that have been published in eight countries and shortlisted for the PEN Center USA Fiction Prize and Canada's Scotiabank Giller Prize, among others, and is co-editor, with Daniel Hahn, of the forthcoming *Penguin Book of Brazilian Short Stories.* Viswanathan is professor of creative writing at the University of Arkansas in Fayetteville.

CHIMAMANDA NGOZI ADICHIE is an internationally acclaimed novelist and essayist. She is the author of six books of fiction and nonfiction; her 2013 novel *Americanah* won the National Book Critics Circle Award and was named one of *New York Times'* Top Ten Best Books of 2013. She has been awarded honorary degrees from seventeen institutions, and her work has been translated into over thirty languages. In 2015, she was named one of *Time* magazine's one hundred most influential people in the world; and in 2017, *Fortune* magazine named her one of the world's fifty greatest leaders. She is a member of the American Academy of Arts and Letters and the American Academy of Arts and Sciences.